101
Ways to Sell More of Anything to Anyone

ALSO BY ANDREW GRIFFITHS

101 Ways to Market Your Business
101 Ways to Advertise Your Business
101 Ways to Really Satisfy Your Customers
101 Ways to Boost Your Business
101 Ways to Have a Business and a Life
101 Ways to Build a Successful Network Marketing Business
101 Secrets to Building a Winning Business

COMING SOON

Recession-Proof Your Business Now

101
Ways to Sell More of Anything to Anyone

Sales tips for individuals, business owners and sales professionals

Andrew Griffiths

ALLEN&UNWIN

First published in 2009
Copyright © Andrew Griffiths 2009

All rights reserved. No part of this book may be reproduced or transmitted in any form or by any means, electronic or mechanical, including photocopying, recording or by any information storage and retrieval system, without prior permission in writing from the publisher. The Australian *Copyright Act 1968* (the Act) allows a maximum of one chapter or 10 per cent of this book, whichever is the greater, to be photocopied by any educational institution for its educational purposes provided that the educational institution (or body that administers it) has given a remuneration notice to Copyright Agency Limited (CAL) under the Act.

Allen & Unwin
83 Alexander Street
Crows Nest NSW 2065
Australia
Phone: (61 2) 8425 0100
Fax: (61 2) 9906 2218
Email: info@allenandunwin.com
Web: www.allenandunwin.com

National Library of Australia
Cataloguing-in-Publication entry:

Griffiths, Andrew, 1966–
101 ways to sell more of anything to anyone/Andrew Griffiths.

ISBN 978 1 74114 788 9 (pbk.)

Selling.
Selling—Handbooks, manuals, etc.
Selling—Vocational guidance.

658.85

Set in 12/14 pt Adobe Garamond by Midland Typesetters, Australia
Printed in Australia by McPherson's Printing Group

10 9 8 7 6 5 4 3 2 1

Contents

Acknowledgments	xi
Preface	xiii
Introduction	xv
Doing business today	xv
New era customers—they have more choice	xv
Get over the fear of becoming a used car sales person	xvi
If it's not worth selling then don't sell it	xvii
The ten biggest and most common sales mistakes	xvii
How to use this book to sell more of anything	xviii
The power of being extraordinary	xix
Section 1: It's all about attitude	**1**
# 1 Decide what type of sales person you want to be	2
# 2 A good sale is more important than just a sale	3
# 3 The best sales people are patient, persistent and polite	4
# 4 Believe in your product—it shows if you don't	6
# 5 Commit to constant and neverending self-improvement	7
# 6 You have the sale already—it's up to you not to lose it	8
# 7 Honesty, integrity and passion—the three pillars of successful selling	9
# 8 Never judge a man by his clothes	12
# 9 Become a listening guru	14
# 10 What is your attitude to money?	17

101 WAYS TO SELL MORE OF ANYTHING TO ANYONE

	Section 2:	Getting prepared to sell	21
	# 11	To succeed at sales you need goals	23
	# 12	Product knowledge, a sales person's most powerful tool	25
	# 13	Give your customers the most compelling reasons to buy your products	27
	# 14	Know everything about your competitors	28
	# 15	Promotional material can make or break a sale	29
	# 16	Rehearse your sales presentation	30
	# 17	Look the part or go home	32
	# 18	Be prepared and have everything at your fingertips	34
	# 19	Always be ready to make a recommendation	35
	# 20	Tell me in thirty seconds or less why I should buy from you	37
	Section 3:	Opportunities to sell are everywhere	41
	# 21	Never be afraid to ask for a lead or a referral	43
	# 22	Don't listen to the cynics	45
	# 23	Be careful what you say	46
	# 24	Read the newspapers, watch the news	48
	# 25	Check under your nose	49
	# 26	Build your reputation and leads will come to you	51
	# 27	Keep a notebook with you at all times	52
	# 28	Walk in and say hello	53
	# 29	Go back over the old customer records	54
	# 30	Get your head around networking and what it can do for you	56
	Section 4:	Presenting your product	61
	# 31	Do something memorable	62
	# 32	Treat everyone like a decision-maker	64
	# 33	Do your homework on the client	65
	# 34	Adapt to whatever is thrown at you	66
	# 35	Use technology to present your product (to all generations)	68
	# 36	It's always good to get physical	70
	# 37	One size no longer fits all	71
	# 38	Consider the length of your presentation	72

CONTENTS

| # 39 | Breakfast, lunch, dinner or a coffee? | 73 |
| # 40 | Jargon is a passion killer | 74 |

Section 5: Face-to-face selling — 77
# 41	It's okay to be nervous—it means you care	78
# 42	Respect the customer in every way	79
# 43	Become an exceptional observer	81
# 44	Ask questions to get started	82
# 45	Tailor your sales pitch to suit your customers' needs	84
# 46	Beware the robot syndrome	86
# 47	Clarify where to from here	87
# 48	Always have something to leave behind	88
# 49	Write notes to help you remember your customer	89

Section 6: Selling over the phone — 93
# 50	Start at the beginning	94
# 51	Be prepared and have everything in front of you	96
# 52	Get your head right before you pick up the phone	98
# 53	Apply the same principles as for face-to-face selling	99
# 54	It is a numbers game, but quality always outperforms quantity	101
# 55	Leave clever, creative messages	102

Section 7: The challenge of the internet — 107
# 56	Where do businesses go wrong when selling on the internet?	108
# 57	The old principles still apply	110
# 58	Before you press 'send', stop and think	111
# 59	Embrace change—it's not so scary	113
# 60	Use viral marketing	115
# 61	You have only a few seconds to engage and compel	117

Section 8: The art of following up — 121
# 62	Clarify what the customer is expecting from you	123
# 63	Ask the customer when they want you to contact them	124
# 64	Great follow-up takes great organisation	125
# 65	Under promise and over deliver—always	126

# 66	Don't send boring follow-up letters	128
# 67	Never assume—always check that the customer received what you sent	129

Section 9: Closing the sale — 133
# 68	Learn to read the signals that someone is ready to buy	134
# 69	Be brave enough to ask for the business	136
# 70	Act like the sale is a foregone conclusion	137
# 71	Objections are not always bad	138
# 72	Have a win/win philosophy	140
# 73	If it's not going well, get to the real problem	141
# 74	Keep a surprise or two up your sleeve	142
# 75	Very few people are good at closing—make it your mission	143

Section 10: It's a marathon, not a sprint — 147
# 76	Look at the big picture	148
# 77	Remember they are *your* customers!	149
# 78	Often the most difficult customers become your greatest fans	150
# 79	Sometimes you have to walk away	151
# 80	Beware of sales burnout	152
# 81	What to do when you hit a hurdle	154

Section 11: Creating advertisements that sell — 159
# 82	If it doesn't get read, seen or heard it's a waste of time	161
# 83	Big outdoor signs create big impacts	163
# 84	Make people laugh	164
# 85	Use the power of testimonials to supercharge your advertising	166
# 86	Preach to the converted	168

Section 12: Learning a new language — 171
# 87	Learn to tell when your customer is distracted	173
# 88	Look for signs that they either like or dislike what they are hearing	175

| # 89 | Mirroring, a simple technique that will improve your sales skills | 177 |
| # 90 | Don't set off the 'bullshit detector' | 179 |

Section 13: Developing your own style — 183

# 91	Work on your reputation	185
# 92	Become a resource for your clients	186
# 93	Always respect your clients	187
# 94	Be yourself	188
# 95	You can never read enough sales books	189
# 96	Do regular sales training	190
# 97	Grow with your customers	191
# 98	Do what others won't do	192
# 99	Use what you sell	194
# 100	Be detached from the outcome—customers smell desperation	195
# 101	Have an extraordinary amount of fun	197

20 bonus tips to help you sell more of anything — 201

# 102	Send articles from newspapers	203
# 103	Reward people for giving you a lead	204
# 104	Sometimes it pays to 'down sell'	205
# 105	Develop a genuine interest in people—you may be surprised	206
# 106	Ask your customers for their ideas	207
# 107	Visualise the outcome	208
# 108	Be a high quality corporate citizen and tell your customers that you are	209
# 109	Don't be afraid to talk about money	210
# 110	Use food to sell more of anything	211
# 111	Share your life with your customers	212
# 112	Be accessible to your customers	213
# 113	Have a moaning buddy	214
# 114	Is your business customer friendly?	215
# 115	Mystery shop another business	217
# 116	Do a public speaking course	219
# 117	Share company victories with your customers	220

# 118	If you are confident enough, let your customers try your product	221
# 119	Pick up the cost of the call	222
# 120	Make it really easy for people to pay you	223
# 121	Register a clever domain name	224

Where to from here?	227
Recommended reading	228
About the author	230

Acknowledgments

As always there are many people to thank. Writing a book is a production line with some very talented people providing their expertise to make it the best it can be. I would like to thank everyone at Allen & Unwin in Sydney for their enthusiasm, commitment and professionalism. It has been a wonderful journey with many more twists and turns ahead I'm sure.

There is one person I would like to say a special thank you to. He has always been there, constantly applying pressure with gentle questions like 'Where is that damn manuscript?' and assurances like 'No, we don't believe that a crocodile ate it'—Mr Ian Bowring, my publisher at Allen & Unwin. Ian has worked on every single book in the series and while the process has aged him terribly, his neverending support has helped to make this series the success it is.

I have also had the pleasure of working with truly exceptional sales people. They have sold everything imaginable (and some things that we really don't even want to imagine). In no specific order, but with much appreciation, these are my sales gurus: Gerard Obersky, Neil Swann, Tom McPartland, Bob Baldwin, John Mason, Bruce Dillon, Todd Parker, Matt McKinlay, Julie Stokes, Karen 'Shiner' Andrews, Julie 'Bismarc' Mahoney and the truly magnificent Sarah 'Success Through Sales' Fraser.

And I doubt that I would even be here if it weren't for Mr and Mrs Devin (Les and Jan). Thank you for the love and affection that you showed me at a very challenging time. You may not realise what you did, but you saved me.

And then there's my editor, fan club leader and all round cheeky little thing—Dr Debra Lawson. Thank you, thank you, thank you.

Enough of this mushy stuff, let's get selling.

Preface

This is the eighth book that I have written in the *101 Ways* series and it covers the vitally important topic of selling. I have written it to help any business sell more of its products or services, regardless of which industry it may be in or where it is located geographically. Most of my readers are predominantly small business owners or managers, but this book is relevant for anyone who has to sell anything and, let's be honest, that's pretty much all of us these days. Like the other books in this series, this one is written in a very simple, no-nonsense, practical style designed to give immediate answers to any issues that you may be facing. At the same time I aim to provide a broader perspective on the world of sales.

There are many books written about the new concepts and ideas revolving around selling and there are some fabulous books on innovative sales techniques for specific industries. The difference with *101 Ways to Sell More of Anything to Anyone* is that the hints, tips and advice it provides are timeless. It deals with what some people call the fundamentals. These fundamentals may not be as flashy as some ideas, they may not be the topic of the latest workshops doing the rounds, but I guarantee they work—following them will increase the amount of sales you can generate and they can be adopted by anyone in a few minutes.

I am often asked what's the best thing to do to make a

business more profitable. Most of the time my response is the same: learn how to sell. Sounds obvious doesn't it? But the reality is that most businesses don't sell: they simply collect money. If you can learn how to sell, or if you can improve your sales skills, your business will become one of a very elite few. You will certainly make a lot more money and you will attract many new customers—those people looking for skilled sales professionals who can help them make their purchases.

I aim to avoid using jargon as much as possible. Selling really isn't complicated yet there is an almost mythical aura surrounding it and sales people in general. I think we have turned something simple into something very complex and I am not sure why. Selling anything is simply a matter of treating your customers with respect, listening to what they want and then making it as easy as possible for them to buy it from you. Doing it better involves being a better communicator and a more acute observer of people. Hence I don't believe that some people 'just aren't cut out to be in sales'. I think we all can sell; we simply need to develop our own style, to become better at listening to our customers and, most importantly, to learn to give them what they want.

In various incarnations I have sold a lot of different things. My first sales job was selling newspapers on the streets of Perth at the age of seven. Since then I have sold everything from encyclopaedias door-to-door to advertising, both as an employee and as a business owner. I have learnt a lot about people and selling in general. I will share as many of my own experiences and observations as possible in the hope that these real-life examples will really hit home for you.

I hope you enjoy reading and using *101 Ways to Sell More of Anything to Anyone*.

Andrew Griffiths

Introduction

Doing business today
There is little doubt that the world has become a whole lot more complicated in the last ten to fifteen years. Likewise doing business has become more complex on just about every level. There was a time when if you had a pie shop, all you needed to do was get up, make pies, sell pies and go home. Today we have to be part marketing guru, part human resources manager, and at times a personal coach, an accountant, or even a lawyer and then we need to be a sales professional. This may sound overly dramatic but most people I encounter tend to agree.

We live in a world filled with competition. Many of us find ourselves selling the same product or service, fighting for the same dollar. Competition is here to stay and will only keep increasing, so we all need a point of difference. Customers today are much more demanding and educated so I believe that being able to sell effectively is a fantastic point of difference for any business, simply because sales skills are generally shocking and getting worse. Good selling skills have become more important and more relevant than ever before.

New era customers—they have more choice
As customers we are more informed than ever before. The advent of the internet has put information about anything we

can think of (and some things we thankfully could never think of) at our fingertips. As a result, we know we have more choice and we are not afraid to make use of it. We were all a little nervous the first time we booked a flight or a hotel online. Not any more—now it is second nature. Imagine what impact this online world will have on us in ten years' time.

We are living in the era of communication. We talk, we send text messages, we email, we call, we fax (less often but it's still an option) and we spend time in online worlds. We ask our friends for advice when thinking about making a purchase and we look for security by asking someone who has purchased something similar because we don't necessarily believe everything we read. As customers we have become more demanding in every way. We have more complex needs, and we want more and more.

But there is an upside to this huge increase in communication—if you develop a reputation for being able to meet, and ideally exceed, your customers' expectations, they will find it easy to promote you and your business and you will have a constant stream of new customers heading your way. I have witnessed this happen time and time again.

Get over the fear of becoming a used car sales person
Many people have a real fear of being perceived as being a pushy or high-pressure sales person. They may hide behind this 'fear', using it as a convenient reason for not participating in sales training or taking any responsibility for sales within an organisation.

I hear the words 'I'm not in sales so I don't need to know about selling' all the time. Well I hate to burst anyone's bubble, but the reality is that we are all selling something. It might be our products and services, it might be the company we work for, or it might just be ourselves in a job interview or on a date. Today no one is isolated from selling in some shape or form and if you are employed by a company, you share the respon-

INTRODUCTION

sibility of selling and promoting that business whether you think you do or not.

If it's not worth selling then don't sell it
A lesson I learnt very early on in my sales career is that if you don't believe in what you are selling then don't sell it. If you sell something that you believe is not as good as it should be, is overpriced, or is faulty or defective in any way, it will always come back to haunt you.

Personally I find it impossible to sell anything that I don't believe in 100 per cent. Be selective about what you decide to sell and make sure you believe in it. If you want to start a business, please take the time and the energy to research whatever you plan to sell to make sure it is something you believe is worth selling.

The ten biggest and most common sales mistakes
Trying to narrow this list down to ten was a challenging task. However, based on my observations and experiences, these are the biggest and most common mistakes a sales person can make:

1. Not being prepared when it comes to making a sales presentation, either face to face—as in a retail environment—or over the phone.
2. Not looking the part—where the sales person is dressed inappropriately or the entire sales environment looks unprofessional and unappealing to the customer.
3. Not having enough knowledge about the products or services being sold. This is a big issue and in fairness to sales people around the world, the rate of product development is making it really hard to keep up. But we have to, because out customers not only expect it, they deserve it.
4. Not asking the right questions. Selling is about communicating and a big part of being a successful communicator

is being good at asking the right questions so you can find out exactly what your customer needs.
5. Not listening to what the customer is saying. This goes hand in hand with not asking the right questions and being a poor communicator. Poor sales people never listen to the customer.
6. Not getting back to the customer as promised—or in other words, they over promise and under deliver. We all know how frustrating it is when we have to chase sales people.
7. Not having clear, specific sales goals. Very few people set goals but those that do tend to achieve them. The same is absolutely true when it comes to selling.
8. Not reading the customer. This means being able to interact with the customer and see that you are connecting with them, that you are helping them and that you are doing your job as a sales professional.
9. Not being compelling. If you don't believe what you are selling, don't sell it. Being compelling generally translates to being believable and sales people already have a stereotype to overcome. If you don't believe what you are saying, your customers won't either.
10. Not caring about the sale. This is the situation where the sales person really doesn't care if the person buys a product or not. They still get paid the same amount so their attitude towards their customers can reflect this. This type of sales person can cost a business a lot of money.

This book will address each of the above issues and many more. Most importantly, it will offer solutions to these problems which will help to increase your sales dramatically.

How to use this book to sell more of anything
There is a lot of information in this book. Some readers may prefer to start at the beginning and work their way through

each section. Others may prefer to scan the table of contents and read a section that feels appropriate to them right now.

Whatever your preferred reading option, it means little if you don't take action. I have left plenty of spaces to write throughout the book. I strongly encourage you to use it as a workbook or your own private sales coach. Read it and then read it again. Leave it on your desk, by your bed, in your bathroom or in your car. Pull it out whenever you get stuck for ideas or inspiration.

Selling can be simple but we all get a little lost from time to time and need inspiration. Use this book and whatever tools you can to help you achieve your goals. I have included a reading list of other sales books that have been very beneficial to me and I am sure they will help you.

The power of being extraordinary

I talk a lot about the power of being extraordinary. The difference between good and extraordinary is often not a lot but, like most things in life, very few people are willing to go the extra mile. The rewards for those who *do* go the extra mile are huge. In the words of the famous Tony Robbins, if you aim for good you get good. Who wants to be good? If you aim for great, you get great. Well that's better, but is it the best? The only real option is to aim for exceptional. I have been fortunate enough to meet some of the most exceptional sales people in the world and they share two traits: a desire to be the best and a passion for what they do.

The final piece of advice that I want to share with you before we get started is to have as much fun as possible when you are selling. Love what you do, be passionate about what you sell and enjoy the rewards that will come your way on every level.

'Nothing can stop the man with the right mental attitude from achieving his goal. Nothing on earth can help the man with the wrong mental attitude.'
Thomas Jefferson

1 It's all about attitude

Great sales people all have a great attitude. If you really want to learn how to sell more of anything, you may need to make a few changes to your attitude. Perhaps you are on track and just a small tweak here or there is necessary. Or perhaps a complete attitude overhaul is required. Wherever you are in the scheme of things, please believe me when I say your sales success or failure is 90 per cent dependent on what happens in your head long before you get anywhere near a customer.

Read this section with an open mind and be prepared to do what it takes to develop the attitude that will help you become the sales person you truly want to be.

1   Decide what type of sales person you want to be
2   A good sale is more important than just a sale
3   The best sales people are patient, persistent and polite
4   Believe in your product—it shows if you don't
5   Commit to constant and neverending self-improvement
6   You have the sale already—it's up to you not to lose it
7   Honesty, integrity and passion—the three pillars of successful selling
8   Never judge a man by his clothes
9   Become a listening guru
10 What is your attitude to money?

#1 Decide what type of sales person you want to be

We all know the corny clichés about sales people being smooth, silver-tongued, slick and basically dishonest sharks. Thank goodness the days of the smooth-talkin' shark are long gone, or at least well on the way out—no one wants this type of person selling to them, and who wants to be a pushy sales thug anyway?

It's up to you to decide what kind of sales person you want to be. You need to make a conscious decision, up front. You get to set the rules. For me, I realised long ago that I had a number of goals and objectives when it came to my sales career. They are:

1. I can only sell something that is high quality and that I have confidence in.
2. I will always be 100 per cent honest in my dealings.
3. I will do everything in my power to ensure that my reputation is continually built on positive action.
4. I will only sell for ethical and honest companies.
5. I have to be passionate about what I sell.
6. I want to be proud of every sales interaction that I have.
7. I will be one of the best sales people in whatever industry I am in.
8. I will constantly learn how to be a better sales person.
9. I will be creative and innovative, learning from those around me but never getting stuck in the 'that's the way we always did it' head space.
10. I will always exceed my sales budgets.

I strongly advise that you decide what kind of sales person you intend to be. Or if you have been selling for a long time, decide what are your 'rules' when it comes to selling. Defining these helps to give perspective to what you do, regardless of whether you work in sales or own your own business.

#2 A good sale is more important than just a sale

There used to be a consensus among sales people that a sales person should do whatever it took to get a sale. I don't necessarily agree with this. I think it is more important to make a good sale rather than just make a sale. So what is a good sale?

For me a good sale is one where everyone wins. The customer's needs and expectations are met and ideally exceeded. They get real value for money, the product they purchase will meet their needs, and the interaction is friendly and enjoyable. The business sells a product, makes a profit on it and creates another happy customer who will tell their friends and colleagues about the business. The sales person notches up another sale, earns their money and perhaps a commission, learns some more about selling and acts with honesty and integrity.

These types of sales will pay big dividends in the future. Long-term relationships are built on these win/win encounters. Unfortunately, not all people think this way. The instigator of a problematic relationship can be the sales person, the business owner or the customer. The sales person can bend the truth to get the sale. They can be pushy and act without integrity and make promises that will never be delivered on. The business can sell inferior quality products or services, at inflated prices, with lots of small print designed to trick the customer. And speaking of customers, many of them can be really difficult to deal with. They can be ridiculously demanding and rude, or have no understanding of commercial reality so they screw you until you can't possibly make any money.

Generally it only takes one of the three players to cause problems for the whole deal to fall over, or for a clean sale to become a dirty one. We all play a role in this process. I suggest that you do your part to make a 'good' sale rather than just making a sale.

#3 The best sales people are patient, persistent and polite

Being a sales person for most of my life, albeit in various shapes and guises, I have no doubt that the best sales people in the world are patient, persistent and polite. Don't be fooled into thinking that people who have the gift of the gab make the greatest of sales people—they don't.

Patience is a wonderful quality in a sales person, particularly today. There is so much information being dispersed today that it is really hard for customers to sort it all out and to make an informed decision. That is why many of them like to collect information and then process it. No amount of pushy selling is going to convince them otherwise.

I have spent years working on potential clients, hoping to win them over. I have been very patient and it has generally paid off, regardless of which industry I was in. I made a point of letting them know I was there, that I was patient and that I would be working to get their business over the next few years. I would make sales calls to these businesses year in, year out, until finally they would give me a go. From there I knew that, as long as my company delivered, this account could grow and grow dramatically.

Most sales people take a short-term approach to selling—get the sale now and move on. This is a short-sighted approach. Those who take their time will succeed—it is only a matter of time.

Next comes persistence. It is important not to become a stalker, but to let the customer know you are not going to give up easily. I have a very close friend who has been selling advertising in publications for years. Tom is an old-school salesman and his results speak for themselves. He wrote the book about persistence and I am constantly amazed at how this pays off for him. If he says he will get a new business to advertise he will. It might take a year or two, but he always gets his customer. How does he do it?

Well, this is where the third part of this tip comes into play: he is extremely polite. He is also a mad Irishman, which of course does help as he has a great sense of humour, but no matter how irritated, fed up, mucked around, lied to or abused he gets, he never, ever gets grumpy or loses his cool when he is with the customer.

Over the years I have had sales people swear at me, throw things, smash the desk, kick tables on the way out, slam doors, abuse my staff and even literally beg for the sale, simply because I have said no to them. Well, doing all of that certainly won't encourage me to do business with them. Never, ever lose your cool with your customers no matter how much work you have put into the sale. If you leave the door open the potential customer is just that—still a potential customer. If you slam it shut, you have to wait for people to leave the company before you can go back to try to sell them anything.

Be patient, be persistent and be polite—always.

#4 Believe in your product—it shows if you don't

I find it impossible to sell anything I don't believe in. This lack of belief in a product can be about it not doing what it promises, the quality of the product, the value for money, and so on. Any good sales person needs to believe absolutely in the product they are selling.

If I am interviewing someone for a sales position and most of their questions relate to the product being sold, the quality control processes, the after-sale service offered by the business, et cetera, I know they are professionals and that they know what they are doing. If all they want to know is when they will get paid, I generally get a different picture of their ability and their integrity in the sales world.

If you have doubts about a product or service that you are charged with selling you need to resolve them, and quickly. If you can't resolve your doubts, perhaps you should be looking for something new to sell. That is certainly what I would do. Customers can tell if you are trying to sell them something that you don't believe in. If you own your own business and your sales people lose faith in your business's products, sales will fall and a fast downward spiral could occur.

One of the best ways to build confidence in your products is to talk to happy customers. I cover following up on a sale later in the book, but if you spend some time talking to existing customers about what they like (and don't like) about what you sell, your confidence will grow. And if there is more bad news than good news, you certainly want to know about it so that you can do something about it pronto.

#5 Commit to constant and neverending self-improvement

This book covers the real fundamentals of selling, the key skills that used to be considered simple and elementary. However, my ideas are based on my experiences in the world of sales. I have never done a single sales course or any external training in the area of sales. What I have done is read hundreds of books written by the leading sales and communication people in the world (sadly many have passed away). I pored over these books, applied the principles they shared and pondered the questions they raised. I read books on all types of selling, sometimes industry specific, sometimes nationality specific, mainstream and niche.

As I read and learnt more I set about putting this newfound knowledge into practice. Every day I learnt more and applied more. My selling skills got better and better and my confidence grew. I came to believe that I could sell anything and be very successful at it, regardless of what it was, as long as it fitted into my personal sales rules as outlined in tip #1.

There is a massive amount of information available on selling. Immerse yourself in it once you have the fundamentals well and truly mastered. Do some training seminars, push yourself and learn from every interaction. Take the time to review each and every sale—what did you do well? What could you have done better? But most importantly of all, commit to constantly becoming the very best sales person you can.

#6 You have the sale already—it's up to you not to lose it

Selling is a mind game. Why do people sell record amounts one week and nothing the week after? From my experience it generally has very little to do with the product being sold and everything to do with the level of confidence and the attitude of the sales person.

I think that all too often the sale is within our grasp and we simply mess it up. People are busy and while at times they may simply be doing some price checking or preliminary research, more often than not they want to buy the item they are talking to you about.

I have always approached a presentation with a very clear belief. I believe that the sale is already mine so long as I carry out the right steps and follow through appropriately. I have enough confidence in my products and services, I know they are very high quality, so why wouldn't the customer want to buy from me? I actually visualise the contract being signed or the cheque being handed over. I spend a few moments clearing my mind, thinking about the presentation or the meeting and visualising how I want it to go. More often than not, that is the way it goes.

Now this may sound a little far-fetched but it has certainly worked for me. If I go into a presentation trying to convince the person to buy something from me, I know I can start to sound almost desperate. No one buys a thing from someone who is desperate. But when I go into a presentation organised, calm and confident and with the internal belief that I already have this sale, I simply need to do the right things not to lose it.

Are you going into your sales environment trying too hard to get the sale? Remember, you already have it—the trick is not to lose it. Believe me, if you can change your attitude, you will definitely see an increase in sales.

#7 Honesty, integrity and passion—the three pillars of successful selling

If you can't sell a product openly and honestly then you shouldn't be selling it. Being honest doesn't just mean telling a customer the facts about a product or service and ensuring that all of the relevant and important information is communicated effectively. It also means being honest about when things will be done, when the product will arrive, what to do if there is a problem and so on.

Unfortunately I seem to encounter a lot of dishonesty in sales, not in what people are saying but in what they don't say. Most misleading information is in the small print and it's not until we want to get out of a contract, or return a product, that we find out exactly how misled we have been. It is easy to say buyer beware, but I think that is just a cop-out. I believe the authorities in every country should tighten up on the small print that we all have to deal with and try to decipher.

If your product or service has weaknesses when compared with your competition, your job is to figure out how to make the most of its virtues without tampering with the truth. Honest sales people build long and prosperous careers. I know many; they are impressive people who enter every sale with the intention of building a relationship with the client that will last for decades. As a result, they sell a lot.

A great sales person has absolute integrity. They know what is right and what is wrong—there are no shades of grey. Anyone who sells anything will at some stage of their career have their integrity tested. It may be by a boss, it may be by a supplier, it may be as part of your own business. You are tested at that moment when you know that what you are contemplating or being asked to contemplate is wrong. Which way will you go? Will you leave a job if your boss asks you to do something that you believe is wrong? Will you tell the customer about the flaw in the discounted product that they are buying?

My integrity, and subsequently my reputation, mean more to me than just about anything else in my professional world. There have certainly been times when my integrity has been tested. Had I gone down that path I could have made a lot more money, but I wouldn't have been able to walk down the street and hold my head high, or sleep at night. If you find yourself in a position where your integrity is being challenged, alter that position as fast as you can. Your job can change, the products or services that you sell can change, but your reputation is yours for life and you decide what that reputation is going to be.

Last but not least is passion. Personally I don't know how anyone can sell anything they are not passionate about. I know that some things are more exciting to sell than others, but luckily we are all different. There are people who are incredibly passionate about selling paper clips. There are people who leap out of bed in the morning to sell toilets. They are lucky; they have found their passion in the world of sales.

It is really hard to sell anything that you don't either believe in or feel passionate about. The wonderful thing about sales is that you can apply the fundamental skills to virtually any product or service. Become an exceptional sales person and you will never be without a job. But having a job and loving your job are two different things. Perhaps when people say they aren't into selling, they just haven't found the right product or service.

Passion is contagious. People love dealing with people who are passionate. We like getting excited about making a purchase and when you encounter a sales person who clearly loves what they are selling it is very hard to say no to them. Added to this is the fact that passionate people go out of their way to find out as much as they can about the product they are selling. They don't find this a chore as they have a hunger to learn, which means that doing research never feels like work.

Honesty, integrity and passion together create a truly exceptional sales person, whether they work in their own business or for someone else. If you want to be the best sales person you possibly can, then be honest and passionate and show integrity and I guarantee the results will be astounding.

#8 Never judge a man by his clothes

A few years back I was presenting a seminar to about a hundred people in Alice Springs, a desert city in the middle of Australia. The crowd was very warm and welcoming and while I spoke to them about the way to build a dynamic business I noticed a man at the front of the room who seemed very excited. He was wearing a pair of tattered shorts, a smelly old singlet and he was barefoot—none of which is considered normal attire even in Alice Springs—and I assumed he was a little strange. I also assumed that he had no money and that perhaps he was mentally challenged in some way. Subconsciously I probably made many more assumptions about this man. We all do it. We form an opinion of a person in a matter of seconds. Sometimes it's right and sometimes it's completely wrong, as I soon found out.

At the end of the seminar this odd man came over to me and started to chew my ear off. He was nice enough, but I didn't really know what he wanted or what he did. We had a pleasant chat, he seemed satisfied and he wandered off, to my relief. A little later the event organiser and I were having a debrief on the night. I had a bit of a chuckle as I told her about the strange little man and she told me he was the richest man in Alice Springs. He was worth tens of millions of dollars and he was a self-made property developer.

I have experienced this same thing many times in my life. Looks can be deceiving and when it comes to selling anything, judging people by their looks can be a sales disaster. I would go one step further and say that often the people we assume are the wealthiest, because of what they are wearing or driving, are often the people with the most debt. A smart sales person will overcome their initial and instinctive desire to judge a person by their appearance and put them in a pigeon hole; that is, they are rich, they are poor, they are a time waster, they will never buy this. They will treat everyone exactly the same and this is what makes them different.

IT'S ALL ABOUT ATTITUDE

I spend a lot of time dressed in suits and travelling. On the weekend or if I am having a day off in a city I like to dress down. I know for a fact that when I walk into most shops wearing an expensive suit, I get served almost immediately and I am generally lavishly looked after by the sales people. But if I turn up in a pair of jeans and a T-shirt, the level of service is completely different. Most of the time I am ignored, even though the amount of money in my bank account is exactly the same.

Break the habit of judging a person by their appearance and treat everyone as equal. Do this and you will sell more of anything to anyone. As a beautiful by-product, you will get to meet and connect with some truly spectacular people whom you may have previously written off.

#9 Become a listening guru

One of the first sales gurus I looked up to was Dale Carnegie, the man who became a legend for classic books including *How to Win Friends and Influence People.* In his very simple and unassuming manner he works through many extremely valuable techniques for becoming a better communicator. Ironically one of his most important observations is that the world's greatest communicators are exceptional listeners and I agree wholeheartedly.

Today we live in a crazy, fast-paced world. We are the centre of our own little universe and, in more ways than one, it is all about 'me'. People tend not to listen as well as they could, simply because they are preoccupied with a million other things.

If you want to improve your sales immediately, learn to listen. Customers desperately want people to listen to them. They want to be able to explain what it is they want and they hope that the sales person they are talking to can provide what they want. How many times have you ordered something only to have it arrive and find that it is wrong? And the reason it is wrong is that the sales person simply wasn't paying attention when you made the purchase.

Becoming a listening guru is the fastest and most effective way to sell more of anything. So how do you do it? First, you have to learn how to ask good questions, those that will give you the information that will enable you to give the customer exactly what they want. For many sales people this is the hardest part. They don't know what to ask, so they let the customer ramble on, hoping that they are explaining their needs. Second, you have to learn to be a great listener. Combine the two skills and not only will your sales success change but so will your life.

I purchased a new car recently. This happened rather suddenly because a friend of mine borrowed my old car and drove it into a ditch. He was okay but the car was a write-off.

IT'S ALL ABOUT ATTITUDE

This meant that I had to go through the dreaded process of buying a new car, interacting with dealers and getting stalked to make a purchase. I set out on a Saturday morning, dressed like I had just come out of the slums of Calcutta, and started doing the rounds of the car yards. Most sales people ignored me, which was my plan, giving me time to look at a number of cars I had short-listed. But sadly once I had looked over the cars, now that I wanted attention, the best I could get was someone pointing towards a brochure rack and telling me to help myself.

My last stop was at an Audi dealership. I thought that these cars would be out of my price range, especially the model I liked, but I went in anyway and got ready to be ignored. The first thing that happened was that I was warmly welcomed by several staff members. Then a salesman came and introduced himself to me and invited me into his office. We spent an hour talking—about me and what I needed in a car. He asked intelligent questions regarding my driving habits, the number of people I carried, the length of the trips that I took, and so on.

At the end of the session he recommended two models. Then he suggested we go for a drive in both to get a feel for them. As we drove, he pointed out the features, basing his conversation on my needs and the information I had given him. He was an exceptional salesman. Both cars were fantastic but I particularly liked the bigger one. At this stage we hadn't even talked price but I ended up buying the more expensive car. I spent $30,000 more than my initial budget and I absolutely love my car. I could have been sold an expensive car at six other dealerships before I got to this Audi dealer but they broke a number of sales rules and didn't even get to first base.

The point I am making here is that what really sold me on this car was the fact that the salesman asked me smart, informed and logical questions and then he listened to what I had to say. Good business sense? Absolutely. I have recommended at least ten other people to this dealership.

Learn to listen, and I mean really listen, and you will convert more sales than you ever imagined. In fact, by being a listening guru you will certainly become a sales guru.

#10 What is your attitude to money?

I used to have a small travel company that sold day tours to people who were visiting Cairns. I would go to the hotels and meet the customers, mostly people on holidays from the UK, and show them brochures on the hundreds of things they could see and do while in Cairns.

My sister used to help me and we always competed good-naturedly with each other. My average sale was about $500 per person. My sister's was about $150. Why the difference? Was I that much better at selling? Not really. Wendy was a very open and honest person, she was a great listener and she was very professional in every way. So what was the difference? I believe that it was because we had different attitudes towards money, even though we grew up in the same environment.

At the time, Wendy was a mother of three kids and her husband was in the navy. Like all young families, money was tight. For her, luxuries were thin on the ground and most of their money went into paying the mortgage and putting food on the table. She would never go out and spend $500 on herself.

I was the complete opposite. I was married but we had no kids. My wife and I loved to spend money on ourselves. We went on holidays, bought nice things, spoiled ourselves often, even if we couldn't afford it. To us spending $500 on something we wanted was no big deal.

So when Wendy was selling tours, she was applying her values and beliefs around money to the sales process; that is, 'Wow, these tours cost a lot of money. I will recommend the cheaper ones.' Whereas my internal dialogue went along the lines of 'These are the very best tours money can buy. I know you will love them and most importantly, they are the ones I would be doing if I were you.'

What are your beliefs about money? What are your staff's beliefs? What does 'expensive' mean to you? What is a lot of money?

Action plan — What can I do right now to become the very best sales person I can be?

IT'S ALL ABOUT ATTITUDE

'*Quality begins on the inside . . . and then works its way out.*'
Bob Moawad

2 | Getting prepared to sell

A great sales person is a prepared sales person. It makes me laugh when I have an appointment booked with someone who is trying to sell me something and they are thirty minutes late. When they finally arrive they are usually dishevelled, sweaty and totally disorganised. They haven't got the brochure for the product they were coming to sell me, they haven't got any business cards, their mobile phone goes off in the meeting and they don't ask me any questions—they simply start blurting out their mentally pre-recorded sales pitch. Then they pack up their bag of tricks, walk out of the office, generally knocking something over on the way out, and I never hear from them again.

How this differs from the true sales professional, who turns up a polite ten minutes early for their appointment. They sit patiently, relaxed and organised. They look smart, they are well groomed and they smile in a friendly way. This same professional has done their homework on my business and they have enough background information to surprise me. They ask intelligent questions, including what I need. They respond with how they can help, specifically, and they advise me clearly on where we go from here. We agree to our next step, they leave the office, having not taken up too much of my time, and they don't knock anything over on the way out.

The difference is all about being prepared. In this section we are going to cover the ways in which you can get prepared to sell.

101 WAYS TO SELL MORE OF ANYTHING TO ANYONE

11   To succeed at sales you need goals
12   Product knowledge, a sales person's most powerful tool
13   Give your customers the most compelling reasons to buy your products
14   Know everything about your competitors
15   Promotional material can make or break a sale
16   Rehearse your sales presentation
17   Look the part or go home
18   Be prepared and have everything at your fingertips
19   Always be ready to make a recommendation
20   Tell me in thirty seconds or less why I should buy from you

#11 To succeed at sales you need goals

I am a huge believer in the power of setting goals. It has worked for me in so many aspects of my life. In recent years I have learnt some new techniques for setting goals from people like Anthony Robbins and Jack Canfield, two of the most dynamic and successful people in the world. I have also spoken to many people, from all walks of life, about their views on goal setting. What I have concluded is that there are lots of different ways to set goals, but that what is important is to do what works for you.

Without a doubt, no goal-setting technique will work without one key ingredient—motivation. For example, if you want a really nice sports car, and you put a picture of it up on the wall (a very effective goal-setting or dream-setting tool for me), this won't achieve much unless you really, really, really embrace the concept of wanting the car. This should extend to the point of visualising driving along your favourite stretch of road in your fantasy car, imagining what it will smell like, what it will handle like, how you will feel at the wheel of your new beast. Simply saying 'I want a Maserati' is unlikely to achieve much, except a hollow feeling when it doesn't materialise.

When it comes to setting and achieving goals, from little ones to humongous ones, I adopt the following techniques, and they always work for me.

1. I am very specific about my goal, as in amounts, dates, colours, etc.
2. I regularly spend time thinking about what it will feel like emotionally to achieve this goal.
3. I put a picture that relates to my goal on the corkboard on my front door, which I walk past several times a day.
4. I think about my motivation for wanting this goal on a regular basis.
5. I never get embarrassed about how big or how personal my goal is. If other people see my 'Dream Board' I don't care.

6. I think BIG. I truly believe I can achieve pretty much anything I set my mind to.
7. I cut out articles, quotes or cards that inspire me to achieve and put them on the Dream Board, in my diary or on the visor of my car.
8. If my goal changes for any reason, I let it go and put up a new goal.
9. I read my goals out loud, often.
10. I read inspiring stories and autobiographies of people who have done amazing things.

Setting goals is just the start. You have to be prepared to get off your butt and make them happen. I intend to buy a Maserati one day, and I know that putting that on my Dream Board will help me to focus on that goal and will certainly help to motivate me, but I will have to do the work necessary to pay for this magnificent car.

To succeed in sales, you need to set specific goals and targets. They need to be realistic but challenging. Time and time again it has been proven that when sales goals are set, people achieve them. In sales, goals are often set for us by others. Whenever I have been in this situation I have always made it my goal not to achieve the targets but to exceed them, and I always did.

#12 Product knowledge, a sales person's most powerful tool

Product knowledge is what you know about the thing you are selling. From my observations, product knowledge is generally really bad. Most sales people simply don't take the time to learn about the products they are selling and this is really frustrating for customers. In fairness, some industries have so many new products coming onto the market that it would be impossible to be completely informed about them all. Tragically, however, many people are simply too lazy to take the time to learn about the products they are selling.

We were in Thailand on holidays a while back and, due to some excessive shopping, we needed to buy a new suitcase to accommodate our purchases. We visited a large department store in Bangkok, which of course had about a million suitcases for sale. A young sales attendant came up to us and using very broken English he ascertained that we wanted a suitcase. We pointed to the ones we liked, and he lined them up and started showing us the features. It was an amazing experience. It took several minutes for him to show us the specific features of each suitcase and he was extremely thorough. He jumped up and down on one to show us how strong it was, he opened every single compartment, and he showed us how to use the locks, the differences between each type of case, the colours available and so on. We chose a suitcase, basing our decision on the recommendations of a salesman who spoke very little English and didn't once mention price. I was blown away.

All too often we ask sales people for advice or technical answers about a product or service and their answer is 'I don't know'. And, what's worse, there is no attempt to even offer a solution. As a result consumers are left to their own devices so they go elsewhere or they go online to research items knowing they will get better answers than they got at the store. The only reason to go back to the first business would be price.

A business that has really knowledgeable sales staff will always stand out from the crowd. And if they promote the fact that they have knowledgeable staff, people will come from far and wide simply because they are desperate for some advice on what to buy.

To succeed at sales we really need to know as much as possible about whatever it is we are selling. Take the time to learn and you will develop a reputation as a leading sales professional and have people clamouring to buy from you.

#13 Give your customers the most compelling reasons to buy your products

We need to identify the reasons that will make a potential customer buy from us instead of from the competition. And these reasons need to be very convincing, or in other words, compelling. Every single business has to have at least one compelling reason for a customer to buy from them. Ideally there should be a lot more than one. Any business owner or sales professional needs to identify exactly what these compelling reasons are. If you can only come up with reasons that are wishy-washy, limp or plain pathetic, then you need to find something more convincing or change businesses.

Once you are clear about what the compelling reasons for buying your products or services are, you need to be able to spell these out for your customers. The reasons may be related not only to the specifics of the product but also to the intangibles. For example, if you sell tyres, you could talk about the features of the actual tyres and why a customer should buy a specific brand, but at the same time you should be able to point to the credibility of the tyre store based on thousands of satisfied customers, awards that the business has won, the guarantee on all work done and so on.

Compelling reasons are what makes you different from your competition (see tip #14). Saying you offer really good service isn't enough anymore. You also need to be able to say, for example, that customers can bring their car in any time for a free tyre check or simply to get the air in their tyres topped up.

#14 Know everything about your competitors

Every sales person needs to know what makes their products different from the competition. To do this you need to do your homework on your competitors. I think some people feel that this is snooping; it may well be but, rest assured, your competitors are more than likely checking up on you too.

So what do you need to find out about your competitors? As much as you can! Find out how their business compares to yours in terms of facilities, the look and feel of their premises, the level of service they offer, what they sell, the prices they charge, their promotional material, their types of customers, their sales skills and so on.

How do you go about finding all of this out? You need to become a detective. Check them out online first of all. Then phone them and ask about a specific product. Go by and make a purchase. Talk to family and friends who may have purchased from them. Talk to suppliers—they often give out far more information than they really should.

Once you have collected the information, do a comparison with your own business. What do you do better than them? What do they do better than you? Look for ways to improve what you do but, most importantly, find out what your competitive advantage is. If you don't know this you are selling blind. This becomes particularly relevant when asked the big question: 'Why should I buy from you?' which is covered in more detail in tip #20.

#15 Promotional material can make or break a sale

Any successful sales person will tell you that having top quality promotional material is a vitally important part of selling your products. I agree. I am a big believer in investing in the very best promotional material you can afford. The material, whether a brochure, a sales presentation folder, a DVD, a website or even a company vehicle, should all be professionally developed, informative and motivational. Nothing looks worse than out-of-date, cheap promotional material. In the scheme of things the cost of high quality promotional material will be small if it helps to sell more of any product or service.

I often hear people saying that their product will sell itself. Well, if that were the case I doubt that every car manufacturer would go the trouble of making very expensive brochures for every model they produce. Of course there are exceptions. Jewellery is one. But in this case, the promotional material is the setting that the jewellery is sold in, the display, the lighting and the emotional aspect of the purchase.

If your promotional material is distributed physically, ensure that your sales staff have plenty of copies and don't be miserly about handing it out.

Emailing electronic brochures is a growing trend. If this is what you do, never send out a Word document. The format will always change. Only ever send out PDF versions of any promotional material. If the last two sentences don't mean anything to you, show them to whoever does your promotional material and they will understand (if they don't they really should).

So what should be included in your promotional material? Great images are essential. Use simple, easy-to-understand language that generally avoids jargon (unless it is needed to sell your product), and provide testimonials from happy customers, instructions on how to buy from you, and relevant contact numbers.

#16 Rehearse your sales presentation

I give a lot of keynote addresses at conferences and special events. I love it and my goal is to become one of the most sought-after keynote speakers in the world. As part of my quest, I have committed to constantly improving and developing my presenting skills.

In the early days, I tended to fly by the seat of my pants. While I was organised about what I wanted to say, I never rehearsed, preferring to figure it out as I went along. This strategy was fine at first, when I was talking to audiences of thirty or forty people. But it wasn't quite as effective when the rooms started to contain four or five hundred people. The pressure of the bigger audiences made it harder for me to think on my feet as there was so much riding on the success of these presentations.

Other professional speakers recommended that I rehearse my presentations, but I felt stupid standing in a room talking to an imaginary group of people. So I didn't do it. Then one day I was booked to present a keynote talk at a conference for leaders in the publishing industry and I felt that this event could be really pivotal to the success of my long-term career. So I planned my presentation, roped in my long-suffering partner as my audience and started rehearsing. And something strange happened—I discovered all of the holes in the presentation, the parts that didn't really flow and the areas that needed more work. I fixed up the bits that needed fixing, called in my 'audience' and did it again. We went through this four or five times before I was completely satisfied.

I went on to give the best presentation of my career in front of approximately 400 people. It was an amazing experience, one that has had a profound effect on my life. I realised that every presentation is important and that if I truly wanted to be one of the greatest speakers in the world, I would need to rehearse each and every presentation.

I believe that if you rehearse your sales presentations they will improve dramatically. Rope in a few friends, loved ones or peers (this is tough and that's what makes it so good) and rehearse your presentation, complete with whatever visual aids you would normally use. I suggest even dressing as you would for your presentation. Give some members of your 'audience' specific questions to ask.

Rehearse, modify and rehearse. It will pay off time and time again and you will develop a reputation as a smart and professional sales person who does impressive sales presentations that achieve results.

#17 Look the part or go home

Some time ago I was a commercial diver. One day I got decompression sickness, a malady that can hit divers for various reasons. My particular case was quite bad and as a result I couldn't dive any more. I was devastated. At the time I was working for a very large Japanese shipping company, and my immediate manager was really committed to ensuring that I retrained and learnt new skills. I was offered a job in sales and marketing for the company. While I didn't really want to pursue this option I took up the offer, mainly because I wasn't sure what else to do. Through a twist of fate, I ended up at a big trade show in Sydney where travel wholesalers came from around the world to buy various Australian-based tour products. I was selling Great Barrier Reef cruises.

Now, I had literally come from working on boats. I was long-haired, scruffy and relatively unkempt (as was the norm when spending weeks at sea). I was determined not to change because I didn't want to become 'just another suit'. I decided that people would have to accept me for who I was. I turned up for the first day of the trade show in a pair of jeans and a T-shirt, looking like I had just fallen out of bed. I set up my booth, sat behind the desk, and waited for people to come and start buying from me. No one did. Streams of professional 'suits' walked by, took one look and kept on walking, some of them noticeably faster.

Well I sat there for the entire day and I sold nothing. Not a single cruise. I became distraught and confronted what I thought was the truth—that I wasn't cut out for this job. Then I had an epiphany. If I wanted to sell to these people I had to look the part. What signal was I sending them, dressed to retain my 'individuality'? Not a good one. This led to what I call my *Pretty Woman* experience.

The minute the show closed I raced down to the town's biggest department store and searched till I found a rather elderly, impeccably dressed, friendly looking salesman. I told him my story and I told him I wanted to become a really successful sales professional. That was all he needed to know. A flurry of activity followed that had me trying on suits, submitting to the ministrations of a tailor who was called in to make adjustments on the spot, buying shirts, shoes, a briefcase and a host of ties, having my hair cut, even getting a manicure. It cost me thousands but I surrendered to the experience and I put my future in the hands of this old man.

The transformation was mind blowing, particularly for me. From the minute I arrived at the trade show the following day I started selling and people were receptive. I felt fantastic, I was confident, I was funny, and I looked like a million bucks. I sold about $6 million worth of cruises that day.

Two things had changed monumentally—my attitude and my appearance. Both were equally important. Since then, I have been a big advocate of the importance of looking the part in whatever sales role you are in. Be proud of your appearance, dress for the market you are selling to (for example, don't wear a suit if you are selling to farmers) and invest in your appearance. Look the part and reap the rewards.

#18 Be prepared and have everything at your fingertips

There is nothing worse than the sales fumbler. This is the person who seems to be perpetually looking for some vital piece of information or promotional material in the midst of a sales presentation. They never have what they need, they promise to send you the missing information but they rarely do. They are disorganised time-wasters and I have little patience for them.

Show your customers respect by being organised before any meeting. This means having all of the appropriate material, information, details, even a pen, at your fingertips. The number of times I get asked if I have a pen to sign my credit card slip when making a purchase really surprises me.

Always be prepared for random sales encounters and opportunities as well. This means having your business card, brochures or other promotional material, or samples of your products (if appropriate) handy. Now that you are armed, be prepared to give this material out whenever the situation arises. If the situation doesn't arise, give it out anyway.

#19 Always be ready to make a recommendation

I used to own a dive shop where I sold scuba equipment for recreational divers. I was eighteen when I purchased the business, and I had no idea what I was doing. Everything I sold and the way I sold it was a reflection of the methods of the crazy Canadian I bought the store from. His philosophy, and therefore mine, was to have as much stock in the store as possible so that people had a huge choice of everything from fins to tanks.

It wasn't long before I was in financial strife. People would come into the shop, spend time looking around, try on a number of things but rarely buy. Luckily I had a good friend who was a very experienced scuba equipment sales person. He could walk into my shop at any time and sell four out of five people a full set of gear, worth several thousand dollars each. Observing my frustration, he let me into a few secrets. He told me I had too much stock. Customers were confused because there were too many choices. His advice was to carry three lines: a cheap set, an intermediate set and a top-of-the-line set. Next he told me to make sure that all the staff, myself included, used the top-of-the-line gear so we knew just how good it was. Then, when a potential customer came into the shop, we could start with the cheaper equipment, work up to the most expensive, and finish the presentation by saying, 'This is the equipment I use because it is the best.' It worked every time.

This simple change in approach turned my business around. From the first day we adopted the new sales technique we only ever sold the top-of-the-line gear. In fact, periodically I had to send back the cheaper and intermediate lines because they got too old and looked terrible on display. We sold a lot of the great equipment and the benefits were threefold: we made a lot more money with the top-of-the-line gear, we had far fewer problems with this equipment and we developed a reputation for quality.

One of the greatest sales faults is not making a recommendation. Customers are bombarded with choices and they want someone to say, 'This is the best product for you.' Any sales person needs to be able to make a recommendation that is based on the needs of the customer. The better you meet these needs, the happier the customer will be.

#20 Tell me in thirty seconds or less why I should buy from you

I have now talked about a number of ways you can get prepared to sell. We have covered topics like looking the part, being organised, knowing your product, comparing yourself to your competitors and much more.

Somehow, we need to be able to put all of this into a simple, short spiel that will convince someone to buy something from you. In thirty seconds or less you need to be able to answer the question 'Why should I buy this from you?' Some people call this the 'elevator pitch'. Very few people can master it, but if you do you will open many doors that would otherwise be firmly closed to you.

Wishy-washy answers don't work. In fact they have the opposite effect—they make customers get cold feet. An elevator pitch needs to be passionate, emotive, factual and convincing. You need to rehearse it, you need to have variations (or you will start to sound like a parrot) and you need to believe it.

I was recently invited to be a keynote speaker at a conference for the company Pack & Send. During a briefing meeting, one of the senior executives mentioned that they were having some trouble clarifying their elevator spiel. To me it was as clear as day and boldly written next to their logo. 'Pack & Send, we send anything, anywhere.' Said loudly and boldly enough it is most certainly a big statement.

I recently met a very interesting man at a presentation I was doing. When I asked him what he did, he looked me in the eye and said, 'I make people like you become multi-millionaires.' Wow, that got my attention! After getting to know more about him, I discovered that he was a financial planner. As to whether he can live up to his promise, we will see.

If you can't convincingly answer the question 'Why should I buy from you?' in thirty seconds or less, you really need to learn how. An elevator pitch is like a new suit—it takes a few goes at wearing it before we are totally comfortable. Try on a few different suits and get some feedback from those around you. Make it fun but, crucially, make sure you can live up to the pitch you are making!

Action plan—What can I do right now to become the very best sales person I can be?

'Give a man a fish, he'll eat for a day. Teach a man how to sell fish and he'll drive a Maserati.'

A not-so-ancient proverb

3 | Opportunities to sell are everywhere

One of the big issues that all sales people will face at some stage in their career is a lack of people to sell to. These periods can be challenging, especially if you are used to having a constant stream of potential customers knocking on your door. When this 'shift' happens some people go into a tailspin. They lose all motivation and gaze wistfully at the front door, hoping a stream of new customers will come flooding in. Others take it as a call to action and go out and find more customers.

The reality is there are always customers around and there always will be. If you are going to wait for them to come to you, you will have limited success as a sales person. If you go and get them yourself, you will have great success and never be out of a job.

This section deals with ways to find customers even when everyone else says that there are none around.

\# 21 Never be afraid to ask for a lead or a referral
\# 22 Don't listen to the cynics
\# 23 Be careful what you say
\# 24 Read the newspapers, watch the news
\# 25 Check under your nose
\# 26 Build your reputation and leads will come to you
\# 27 Keep a notebook with you at all times

101 WAYS TO SELL MORE OF ANYTHING TO ANYONE

\# 28 Walk in and say hello
\# 29 Go back over the old customer records
\# 30 Get your head around networking and what it can do for you

#21 Never be afraid to ask for a lead or a referral

Some sales people (and many business owners) are almost afraid to ask for a lead or referral. I believe this fear is based on the assumption that if you ask for business, people will think that your business is in trouble. Of course nothing can be further from the truth.

We all need to develop the skill of feeling comfortable asking people to refer business to us. From my experience most customers are really happy to do this, but they need to be asked. It's not a matter of people thinking, 'I won't refer business to them unless they ask me to', but rather that most customers just don't think of it.

The key is to learn how to ask and I find that this is the stumbling block. The approach I recommend goes something like this:

> Hey Susan, thank you for being such a great customer. We really appreciate it. By the way, we are serious about building this business. As we grow we can offer even better prices and a greater range of products and still offer the same high level of service to customers like you. It would mean a lot to me if you would refer us to your work colleagues. Thank you so much for helping to promote us.

This message may be sent as a letter or a card, but personally I think it is most powerful when spoken directly to the person. This sends lots of powerful messages. It is personal, it points out that helping you will benefit them, it says thank you and it is specific. Your request can be designed to suit your business but these are the elements to include:

1. Thank the customer for their business.
2. Tell them you are building the business.

3. Explain what this means to them.
4. Assure them that being bigger won't mean worse service.
5. Be specific about whom you want them to refer to you.
6. Reinforce that it would mean a lot to you personally.
7. Thank them in advance for referring people to you.

Ideally, reward them when they refer people.

When we know how to ask for referrals, everyone becomes a potential referee. Imagine if you asked ten people every day to refer business to you. I wonder how many new customers you would attract. So who can you ask? Everyone. Sure, existing customers are great, but how about family, friends, neighbours, the landlord, your accountant, your staff, your suppliers and anyone else who will listen?

#22 Don't listen to the cynics

I went to a travel industry trade show in Papua New Guinea a few years back. Local tourism operators got together and set up booths at a hotel in Port Moresby to encourage expatriate travel from PNG to Australia. The old hands in the travel game didn't believe there was any business to be had from the show. They just saw it as an annual junket, a chance to party for a few days in a very wild city.

I took this as a challenge. I wasn't going to party—I was going to get business and that is exactly what I did. It's true that the people who attended the show really didn't have the capacity to provide a lot of business, but I made contacts among the other people displaying at the show and chased them for business. During the two days I worked my way around the show I booked over 800 people on Great Barrier Reef cruises. I also found hotel representatives and put together packages that became very successful for many years.

I feel strongly about this point. Be very careful about listening too closely to the naysayers. As soon as people start saying how quiet it is and that the market is a tough one, it almost seems acceptable to stop trying. Well it isn't! I much prefer selling in tough times than in boom times because most of the competition gives up and waits for times to get better before they put any energy into what they do. If I had listened to people around me I would never have published my first book, *101 Ways to Market Your Business*. Now, eight books later and with sales in every corner of the planet, I know I made the right decision.

Be careful who you listen to. There are those who, deep down, may not want to see you succeed or, even worse, may not want you to show them up. Sad, I know, but true. Live to the beat of your own drum. When everyone is complaining about how tough it is, use that time to actually go out and get customers. Be bold, be brave, knock on doors, knock down doors and you will thrive while others struggle to survive.

#23 Be careful what you say

A few years back I became incredibly busy running my marketing company. It was great but I was working ridiculous hours, I had put on a lot of weight, I wasn't exercising and I was heading to an early grave. My business was built on my reputation and virtually all of my clients came to me via word-of-mouth referral.

During those days when I would run into people around town, they would ask me how I was going and I would launch into a tirade about how busy and how stressed I was. I would unleash this standard and somewhat mechanical answer on everyone who asked. Deep down I felt a sense of pride because I was so busy. Then one day I stopped the craziness for a few minutes and had a long hard look at my business. We weren't getting referrals for new work any more. I was shocked. Had the quality of our work slipped? Was the market in bad shape and I just hadn't noticed? Had the competition overtaken us? I was at a loss.

So I pulled out a list of my top twenty referees. These were people I had known for some time and who had all sent me many customers. I phoned them all to ask if there was a problem and why they had stopped referring people to us. They all said something similar: 'Andrew, whenever I see you and ask how it's going you always tell me how ridiculously busy and stressed you are. I don't want to add to your pressure by sending you more customers. You clearly don't need them. And I certainly don't want to see you stressed out and having a heart attack because you feel obliged to look after my referrals.'

This floored me. I realised I needed to change my script. Today when people ask me how I am going I have a much better response. I say something along the lines of, 'Yes we are busy, but we are always looking for quality clients and interesting projects.' It took a while but the quality referrals started to roll in again. And I also noticed a wonderful by-product:

I began to feel less stressed because I wasn't forever telling people how under the hammer I was. The power of speech should never be underestimated.

Are you saying things to people that will stop them sending business your way?

#24 Read the newspapers, watch the news

With knowledge comes opportunity. Great sales people know what is going on in their community. They make the time to read local newspapers, watch the news and collect as much information as they can about the market where they sell. They get to know what people are buying, which companies are growing, which ones are downsizing, what is in demand and what is not. They see who is advertising and what they are advertising. All of this information is readily available and it can provide many leads for the astute sales person.

When I was starting my marketing business I would grab the local newspaper every morning and use it to find at least ten new leads. Without fail they were there every day—I just had to be creative enough to see them and then disciplined and bold enough to follow them up. It paid off handsomely. I do the same thing today, just on a larger scale.

#25 Check under your nose

I had an interesting experience several years ago and it made me realise that many leads are right under your nose.

In my office we used to get regular cross-city deliveries. There was a courier called John who would make deliveries for us several times a day. One day I realised that although he had been coming to our office for almost five years I knew virtually nothing about him. Feeling a little embarrassed about this, I asked him if he had time for a cup of coffee. He agreed and we took a few minutes from our busy schedules and headed to the local coffee shop.

I discovered that John was quite an amazing man. He had been involved in the corporate world in Sydney, but his health had suffered and he had decided that he wanted a sea change and a less demanding job so that he could spend more time with his children as they grew up. Being a courier was perfect for him. He started early, finished early, got to meet nice people and there was no real pressure, especially when compared to his extremely demanding former life. We got to know each other better and I felt a lovely connection with this man.

Over the next few weeks something strange started to happen. Our phones stated to go crazy with a pile of enquiries from new customers. I asked my sales people where the leads were coming from and surprisingly they said from John, the courier. He had become our number one fan and he was going all over town spreading the word about how professional my company was and how good our work was. We were inundated with calls from people wanting new logos, marketing plans and advertising campaigns. It was amazing and I will be forever grateful to my friend John.

Since then I have always made the effort to get to know the people who are in my life on a daily basis, no matter what they do. Apart from the fact that I like getting to know people, it has given me an army of sales generators who promote my business every day. Have you got a John right under your nose, someone who could help you generate a pile of new leads every week?

#26 Build your reputation and leads will come to you

If you are good at what you do and you invest in building your reputation, people will seek you out. I don't think it matters what industry you are in or what your actual job may be. Nothing attracts customers more than a reputation for being the best at what you do. I touch on this in other places in the book and it is one of the key underlying themes. Believe me, when you finish reading you will have all of the advice you need to build a bulletproof reputation, though it does take time. If you are careful you will maintain your reputation forever and it should keep growing stronger.

I treat my reputation as my most prized business asset. I do everything I can to protect it, to develop it and to live up to it. In the words of the exceptional visionary Henry Ford, 'You can't build a reputation on what you're going to do.'

#27 Keep a notebook with you at all times

I am not sure if it is a blessing or a curse, but my brain doesn't seem to switch off very often (unless I have a fishing rod in my hands). I get all kinds of ideas and inspiration at all hours of the day and night. I always keep a notebook handy so I can write down my thoughts the minute I have them because if I don't, I often forget them.

I have notebooks in my car, in my briefcase, in the bathroom, beside the bed, by my computer, in my suitcase and in the kitchen (for some reason I get great ideas when I am cooking). In fact if I was stranded on a desert island, notebooks and pens would be up towards the top of my 'wish list'.

It is one thing to write notes all over the place, but there needs to be a way of sorting out this information and taking action. I put all of these bits of paper in one central place and sort through them regularly. Sometimes I look at a particular note and wonder what on earth I was thinking; other times I realise I have had a gem of an idea that I can action immediately and use in my business.

I have generated a lot of sales of various products and services because of my notebooks. If I am out and about and I see a company that I haven't seen before, or someone gives me a lead when I bump into them in the street, I write down the names and do some research. If I tried to commit all of this information to memory there is no way I could do it.

My notebook obsession has become one of my best sales tools. Perhaps it could help you?

#28 Walk in and say hello

When it comes to generating sales leads there are two approaches: passive and active. Passive is when you sit and hope the phone will ring and active is when you get off your butt and go and chase leads. Clearly I am a fan of the active style. It has worked very well for me and I feel far more in control of my destiny when I take this approach.

One particularly effective way of being active is to simply walk into a business and say hello. That's it. Go in, introduce yourself, and let them know who you are and what you are doing. (Some sales people call this trolling—as in trolling a fishing line behind a boat.) At the same time take an interest in their business and find out what they do. The more people you interact with, the more sales you will get. Selling is often said to be a numbers game and in many ways it is.

You might prefer a more structured approach or what is actually a form of cold calling (or bold calling) where you go into a business to try to sell them something on the spot. This is a tough way to sell anything but some people are very good at it. If you use it as a way to generate leads you may find it very effective. In a couple of hours you can introduce yourself to a lot of businesses and leave a lot of business cards. Sure, many of the people you meet may have no interest in what you are selling, but maybe they know someone who does. Never underestimate the value of taking the time to meet a stranger.

#29 Go back over the old customer records

One Friday afternoon I was contacted by a company that sold and installed garage doors. The owner was distraught because business was so bad. She had a team of sales people sitting around waiting for the phone to ring and she was unable to motivate them to generate new leads.

This business had been operating for almost twenty years and it had thousands of past clients. How could things have got so bad? The business had become complacent about chasing new leads and had not spent a cent on marketing. They left it too long and the phone literally stopped ringing.

But there was another issue that intrigued (and concerned) me: how could they have had so many past customers and not be getting referral work from them? I asked the owner about her sales records and database of past clients. She took me out to a decaying storeroom that was filled with overflowing boxes of completed job cards. There were thousands and thousands of them slowly rotting away. I knew in an instant that this was a gold mine.

Most of the garage doors had been installed in private homes and it was unlikely that past customers would need a new door, but now the business offered a range of other products including kits to mechanise garage doors, pool fences, security lighting and alarms for garages. Most of the past customers would have no idea that these products were available.

So I put together a strategy where, starting with the most recent customers and working their way back through the records, the sales people were going to contact them all and offer them a free lubrication and inspection of the garage doors. The installation team were going to show the sales people how to do this and then the sales people were going to go on the road. While doing the free maintenance inspection they would have the opportunity to sell new products and services to the homeowner.

The concept was great but unfortunately the business owner had left it too late. The debt was too high and sadly the business had to close before the rescue mission could be implemented. I have no doubt that it would have worked if only they had acted sooner.

Many businesses seem to forget their past clients. Do you have a gold mine sitting in archive boxes or computer files? Often all it takes is some creativity mixed with a little perspiration to generate big sales.

#30 Get your head around networking and what it can do for you

Some people don't like networking, others thrive on it. If you want to succeed at sales you really don't have the luxury of not networking. This is where you can generate contacts and referrals that will lead to your next lot of sales.

I think the biggest issue for many people is feeling awkward when they are put in a networking environment: What will I say? I don't know anybody. Will I get stuck with some boring person intent on chewing my ear off?

As advertising becomes less effective we need to take our message to the streets. Networking is a means of face-to-face interaction where we get to pitch our products and services to potential customers. I am a little fussy about where I network, simply because my time is too precious to waste. Some events that are thinly disguised as networking events are really just an excuse for a booze-up. Others are filled with the wrong type of people for my kind of business. Some are so poorly run that you couldn't possibly hope to make a decent contact. Because of this I always do my homework on any networking event I am considering attending. I want to know who will be there, the format of the night, the venue and any other relevant information that will tell me if the event will be valuable or not.

There is no doubt that the more people you meet the more sales leads you will get. But there are lots of different types of networking opportunities—some structured, some informal. My advice is simple:

1. Go to any event prepared to tell people what you do and to ask them what they do.
2. Look for common ground where you may be able to do business together.
3. Always have some business cards and brochures handy.

4. Always carry a notebook and pen to make notes to help you follow up on people you meet.
5. Whenever the conversation stalls, ask open-ended questions such as: Tell me about your industry? How did you end up getting into this industry? Why do you think your products/services are so successful?
6. Circulate—you are there to meet new people. Avoid hanging out with the same people you always hang out with.
7. Don't drink too much.

Embrace networking and you will never be short of sales leads. Just choose your events wisely and always go prepared.

Action plan — What can I do right now to become the very best sales person I can be?

OPPORTUNITIES TO SELL ARE EVERYWHERE

'Real integrity is doing the right thing, knowing that nobody's going to know whether you did it or not.'
Oprah Winfrey

4 | Presenting your product

At long last the time has arrived to present your product to a potential customer. Sometimes just getting to this stage has been a challenge, but the hard work is about to commence.

There is an art to presenting and pitching a product and there have been many books dedicated to the subject. I am going to share a few key ideas here that will help to increase the success of your presentation and get you more sales.

31 Do something memorable
32 Treat everyone like a decision-maker
33 Do your homework on the client
34 Adapt to whatever is thrown at you
35 Use technology to present your product (to all generations)
36 It's always good to get physical
37 One size no longer fits all
38 Consider the length of your presentation
39 Breakfast, lunch, dinner or a coffee?
40 Jargon is a passion killer

#31 Do something memorable

Not so long ago a sales rep came to tell me about a new range of printers. I wasn't expecting to be overly excited by his pitch, but I did need a new high-tech printer. He had done his homework. He had collected information from my office manager about the type of printing we did, the type of machines that we needed, the volume, etc. So he didn't need to ask me a lot of questions. After a few introductory minutes of chitchat, he pulled out an egg timer, the old-fashioned type with grains of sand running through it. He put it on the table and said, 'In the time it takes to boil an egg I am going to give you five extremely compelling reasons to buy this machine from me today.'

He certainly had my attention! I sat back wondering how he would convince me to buy a $10,000 printer in three minutes. He continued:

Reason 1   This printer has been voted the best in its class by 100 of the world's leading companies.

Reason 2   We have customised a package that means you will not spend one cent on maintenance during the life of the printer.

Reason 3   I have calculated that based on your current printing workload this machine will save you $3000 per year.

Reason 4   We have pre-approved a finance package that means you have one low monthly payment for as long as you want the machine and there is no minimum period that you are required to keep it.

Reason 5   I have one in the van outside and an installer ready to put it in and set it up right now. One signature and the deal is done.

Do you think I purchased the machine? Absolutely. And the company lived up to every one of its promises.

PRESENTING YOUR PRODUCT

Most sales people do the same old dreary presentations. They do what they have always done and it is boring and ineffectual. I suggest that you look for ways to make your presentations memorable. Be different, take a risk, and stand out from the crowd.

For the record I asked the sales rep what his conversion rate was. He sold a machine to nine out of every ten people he saw. Now that is impressive.

#32 Treat everyone like a decision-maker

Although he had been rude to my receptionist on the phone when trying to make an appointment and had refused to expand on what he was selling, I agreed to see a very persistent advertising salesman, mainly to stop him bugging the receptionist. When he was led into my office, he turned on his 'salesman's pitch', all sugar and spice—he was very polite, incredibly attentive and his product was quite good. Even though I was wary because my staff had said he had been quite rude, I gave him the benefit of the doubt and decided to buy from him.

After he had left several of my team came in and complained about how he had treated them when he had come into the office for his appointment. He was hostile, overfamiliar and totally inappropriate. That was it for me. I didn't care how good his product was, I didn't want anything to do with him or his company. I rang him and told him, only to receive a torrent of abuse before he slammed down the phone.

If I am not sure about a person I always ask my team what they think. I ask them how the person acted when making their appointment, how they treated the staff. I put a lot of stock in how people treat my staff and I make no allowance for arrogance.

Many a sales deal has been killed because rude sales people treat only the decision-maker with respect. My philosophy is to treat everyone in a business as a decision-maker because, in reality, they all influence the outcome in some shape or form.

#33 Do your homework on the client

I am always impressed when a sales person demonstrates that they have done their homework on me and my business. I am far from impressed when I find that they haven't. Sadly, most sales people fall into the latter category. In this age of the internet there really is no excuse for not doing your homework.

There are lots of reasons to do your homework, not the least of which is that it is a sign of respect. Find out about the people and the businesses you want to sell to. Learn about their products, their history, their vision and their successes and failures. This is without doubt a very good way to build a solid rapport within a few minutes.

Whenever I am going to present to a client, I use a checklist to make sure that I am fully prepared.

1. I review their website.
2. I visit the business to see what it looks like and to make sure I can find it.
3. I phone and ask for copies of brochures and sales material.
4. I talk to my friends and associates to see what they know about the business.
5. I do a Google search on the person I am seeing.
6. I research the industry online to see what other companies are doing.

I like to spend some time investigating the industry online. I do global searches to see what is happening in different continents and I search Amazon.com to see if any relevant books have recently been published.

This may all sound like a lot of work and sometimes it is. But from my experience this hard work really does pay off.

#34 Adapt to whatever is thrown at you

I had to pitch to a potential keynote client recently. I was meeting with the CEO and the management team of a very large company and in many ways this was like an interview for me. I had my presentation on my laptop, ready to go. I had brochures, copies of my books, testimonials from happy customers and anything else that I could possibly think of. I was totally prepared.

As I was led into the CEO's office to set up, I was greeted by a big burly man who introduced himself as the CEO and apologised that he had a crisis at home which he had to deal with immediately. I was flying out that afternoon so I offered to reschedule. He said no, he wanted to talk to me now and asked me to walk him to his car. Leaving behind my briefcase with all its carefully prepared material, and with my arms full of the boxes the CEO had asked me to carry, I found myself doing my pitch in the elevator and in the bowels of the building. I had only a couple of minutes before he drove off. As I stood in the car park wondering how I would find my way back, he stopped, reversed to where I was standing and said, 'You've got the job. Thank you for being accommodating.'

So while I couldn't use all my prepared material, I dealt with the situation in the best way I could. I have learnt from many keynote speaking jobs that things do go wrong. Projectors blow up, presentations get lost, microphones stop working, fire alarms go off, and people pass out. Sometimes things just happen, but the key to success is to be ready for whatever gets thrown at you.

Whenever I am to present at a conference I am ready for any contingency. It gives you a great sense of calm and confidence knowing that however the event unfolds you will do your best.

The same applies in any sales presentation. Be prepared, think it through, be organised enough to allow for contingencies and you will be much more successful. If you are too rigid and you fall apart when things start to go wrong, look out. Presenting to people in their space is not an exact science.

#35 Use technology to present your product (to all generations)

We have some amazing technological tools at our disposal these days and they can really help us to sell our products. We can play DVDs on our laptops, link to live websites, do impressive PowerPoint presentations and make really interesting and stimulating pitches to prospective clients.

I think we should all be using technology a lot more and we should be using it to target all age groups and customer types. However, do not use technology for technology's sake. Only use it to enhance the presentation of your product. Trying to impress someone with a flash laptop and lousy PowerPoint presentation simply won't work.

While we need to know how to incorporate technology into our sales pitches it should not make up the whole pitch. Recently, two media reps came to my office to sell me some advertising packages. They arrived looking very formal and we had a moment or two of chitchat. Then they opened up a laptop, pressed play, and turned the machine towards me so I could watch the presentation. As soon as it stopped they closed the machine, said 'Thank you' and 'Call us if you want to book a package' and walked out. I sat there stunned for a while not really knowing what to think. As in this instance technology can become a crutch and can create lazy sales people.

We need to use technology so we need to invest in it. This investment comes in three specific areas. We have to buy good equipment. We have to learn how to use it and we have to use experts to help us create the right presentations. All too often sales people have the first two locked in but then they produce their own presentation which looks terrible.

Last but not least, rehearse with your equipment and programs. A lot of sales reps have come to me and started setting up their presentation with bells, whistles and dancing girls and then, due to a 'technical glitch', haven't been able to continue and we have had to actually talk. These presentations are always a let-down because you have anticipated something big and bold and instead you get something small and light-weight, unless of course they are very good sales people who can recover from the 'glitch'.

#36 It's always good to get physical

It is great if you can get tactile in a presentation. Now I don't mean you should get physical with the customer but I do mean there should be things to hold, handle and interact with. When I was in the diving industry every sales presentation was like that. It was always great when a sales rep came in because you knew there would be boxes of new equipment to paw, try on, play with and generally interact with.

If you can develop ways for people to have physical interactions with whatever you are selling you certainly increase your chances of success. I know that some of you are going to be sitting there wondering how you can make your insurance pitch tactile. Well, there are always solutions—you just have to be creative. When I was first starting out in business, a door-to-door insurance salesman turned up at my office carrying a suitcase. I was intrigued so I let him do a presentation and it was incredibly theatrical and creative. In his suitcase he had fire alarms, stethoscopes, handcuffs, x-rays and a pile of other items that he would pull out when talking about the various types of insurance I just had to have. It was extremely effective and a lot of fun. If only more people sold insurance like this today.

Give your potential customers products, props, food, sounds and anything else to get them involved in the presentation. It will have a much bigger impact than just talking at them and you will most certainly develop a reputation as an extraordinary sales person.

#37 One size no longer fits all

It is essential that you tailor presentations to suit the business or the customer you are presenting to, regardless of whether it is an electronic presentation or a printed presentation or even over the phone.

Remember, it is all about them, not you. Think about the presentation from their perspective and put yourself in their shoes. Put their company name in the presentation wherever you can. Show that you have taken the time to customise your pitch to what they need, not what you want.

We live in a world that emphasises our right to be treated as individuals. Respond proactively to this and you will have far greater success in the sales arena. The days of making just one presentation to suit whoever you happen to be pitching to are long gone.

I use very different images depending on who I will be presenting to. I always match the images to the age group of the people I am presenting to and the industry they are in. I buy images online to make the presentation look very professional and current. Sure, it takes a bit longer and costs a few bucks to buy the images from iStockphoto.com, for example, but the end result is far better than if I had to use amateur photographs and illustrations.

My best advice is to treat every single presentation as if it were unique. Treat it like this and your customers will notice and it will certainly increase your chances of getting a sale.

#38 Consider the length of your presentation

How long should your presentation be? This is a tough question and one that really doesn't have a specific answer. It depends on so many variables but I do have a few rules of thumb that guide me when I am planning a presentation.

I think that presentations should be shorter rather than longer. I would much rather do a dynamic, compelling five-minute presentation than a dull, drawn-out one-hour presentation.

I think that a lot of work can be done before the actual presentation to make sure that you do not waste anyone's time. If you do your homework, you will know what to say and what to avoid.

When you enter a room you should clarify exactly how much time the prospective client has and watch the clock closely so that you don't run over time. If the client keeps talking and asking questions stay on but if they start looking at their watch, you need to get their attention back or get out quick.

I always have some sacrificial material. This can be cut out if time runs short or if there is no need for it. But I will include it if the customer is interested and time permits.

Always go for quality not quantity when it comes to doing a presentation.

#39 Breakfast, lunch, dinner or a coffee?

When I am making a time to present to a potential customer, I will do it at any time that suits them—morning, noon or night. Personally I like breakfast presentations. My brain works better in the morning just so long as I have enough caffeine running through my veins. I also find that when they are out of the office people are generally in a better mood. They are relaxed, less stressed and more open about their needs and expectations.

Interestingly enough, I think that today I do more presentations in coffee shops than in boardrooms, perhaps because this is my preference. I have colleagues who like to present over dinner. They like to take their clients out for a meal so that they have their attention for several hours and can pitch in a more relaxed and less time-sensitive manner.

I have also encountered a number of potential clients who want to talk about an idea at the gym or while going for a walk. It's a hard way to do a PowerPoint presentation but it certainly breaks down the barriers!

There are two important issues here. One is to be open and flexible about where and at what time you present. The more willing you are to be flexible the more chance you will have of getting in front of a prospective customer. However, if the customer doesn't have a preference, try to arrange to have the presentation at the time when you function best.

#40 Jargon is a passion killer

Far too many sales people think they will impress a customer by spouting industry jargon. The customer is often too embarrassed to say that they don't know what the sales person is talking about. So they sit there nodding their head feeling resentful and dumb. Not exactly the perfect buying mood is it? The use of jargon drives me crazy and it really says a lot more about the sales person's need to impress than the customer's lack of knowledge.

If you want to sell more of anything, avoid using industry jargon or buzz words as much as possible. Keep your presentations simple, to the point, uncomplicated and factual. Customers are not dumb and the last thing you want to do is to treat them as if they are.

The same principle applies to text in brochures, on websites and in letters—avoid jargon at all costs. Use plain language that everyone understands no matter how unique you think your industry may be. A rule of thumb is that anything you promote should be able to be understood by a twelve-year-old. Why? Because simple sells.

Action plan — What can I do right now to become the very best sales person I can be?

'What you get by achieving your goals is not as important as what you become by achieving your goals.'

Zig Ziegler

5 | Face-to-face selling

While much of the advice in this book applies to face-to-face selling, the tips and recommendations in this section apply specifically to face-to-face interactions.

Face-to-face selling occurs in a lot of different ways. It may be selling behind a cash register, working the floor of a retail outlet, presenting in an office, or in any other situation where you and the customer are in front of each other. I really like having the customer in front of me. I find I can glean information from them when I can see them. Other people find it very challenging and nerve-racking. These tips will help those who are confident as well as those who need a dose of inspiration.

41 It's okay to be nervous—it means you care
42 Respect the customer in every way
43 Become an exceptional observer
44 Ask questions to get started
45 Tailor your sales pitch to suit your customers' needs
46 Beware the robot syndrome
47 Clarify where to from here
48 Always have something to leave behind
49 Write notes to help you remember your customer

#41 It's okay to be nervous — it means you care

I do a lot of keynote speaking these days and I still get very nervous. I thought that after a few years of standing up in front of crowds my nervousness would go away but it didn't, and this bothered me. In an attempt to become a better presenter I started to read a number of books by leading keynote presenters from around the world. I learnt that these amazing professionals, who I thought simply got up and presented in a Zen-like state, also suffered from nerves. Many said that it was this nervousness that made them spend extra time preparing and rehearsing, to ensure that they delivered the best presentation possible. If they didn't care about the quality of their presentation, they wouldn't be nervous. So I have changed my philosophy and embraced this nervousness myself. I always go the extra mile and spend as much time as possible getting organised and preparing for every keynote presentation I do, and I think it shows. I have realised that my nervousness is a good thing and that hopefully it will not go away so I can keep on improving.

I think the same thing applies when it comes to making a face-to-face sales pitch or presentation. If you don't care about the customer or the outcome, it is unlikely you will get nervous. Your customers know this subconsciously. I would much rather have someone present to me who is a little nervous rather than overly confident.

The key here is to manage your nervousness. Play the presentation out in your mind, rehearse it, ensure you have all of your information on hand and let the fact that you care shine through. I really believe that this will pay off in the long run.

#42 Respect the customer in every way

Respect is a powerful thing and one that seems to be getting lost in the sales process. Anyone selling anything, especially face to face, needs to show absolute respect to their customers. Overfamiliarity is irritating and a certain way to kill a sale. So how should we show respect? I follow these rules when selling face to face:

1. I always book an appointment. Turning up unannounced is rarely a good idea.
2. I explain how much time I will need and I keep it as brief as possible, to show respect for their time.
3. I work around the client's wishes—if they want to meet at 7 a.m., I meet at 7 a.m.
4. I leave a contact number in case the client needs to change the appointment for any reason.
5. I make a point of finding out as much as I can about the business before I get there.
6. I arrive early, well presented and organised.
7. If the person I am seeing is older than me, I call them Mr or Mrs, unless they say otherwise.
8. I make a point of not taking more time than I said I would, unless the client specifically keeps me there because they want more information on the spot.
9. I ask intelligent questions and I listen to the answers.
10. I aim to give them what they want. If I can't give them what they want I tell them so on the spot.
11. I advise them of what follow-up action I will be taking and when; for example, if I have to supply a quote, I will tell them when they will have it.
12. I make sure that I get the follow-up material to them before I said I would.
13. I contact the client to make sure they received the follow-up material.

14. Even if they say they don't want my product, I always thank them, promise to keep trying if appropriate and I stay in touch.
15. If the client gives me any confidential information I keep it confidential.

I know some of the above ideas might sound a little old-fashioned, but they work really well for me. It is my 'code of conduct' and I have been using it for over twenty years. Respecting other people is a choice and it does get noticed. Sometimes we need to swallow our ego and that isn't a bad thing. I suggest you work out what respect means to you and come up with your own 'code of conduct' for any situation where you and your customer come face to face.

#43 Become an exceptional observer

Exceptional sales people have exceptional powers of observation. They take the time to observe carefully and then use the information they gather to make logical and smart decisions. When you do a sales call, careful observation is without a doubt one of your best tools. Looking around the waiting room of any office will tell you volumes about the business. It will tell you if the business is prosperous, if the management cares about the staff, if they pay attention to detail, if they respect people.

Train yourself to become an exceptional observer. An excellent exercise is to spend one week observing the world around you. Don't just glance at things; look at them carefully. Take notice of what people in the street are wearing. Notice what colours their clothes and shoes are, what sort of hair they have, how they walk or what they are doing. Read the number plates on cars. Read every single word on a page in the newspaper. Write down what the television commercials were when the ad breaks finish. Note what colour eyes your family and friends have. Look around your local coffee shop—note what's for sale, how much it is, what the signs say. If you do this for long enough you will start to become a better observer. The smallest things will catch your eye, things you wouldn't have noticed before, and the world will seem more colourful and interesting.

So how does this improve your selling skills? It helps you become better at reading people. You can tell a lot by looking at and properly listening to someone. Are they stressed, are they frustrated, are they angry, are they tired, are they ready to buy? All of this information is valuable and important. In Section 12 I talk more about body language and the importance of reading and understanding it.

#44 Ask questions to get started

You can discover a lot by looking at someone's body language and by being a good observer, but nothing beats asking your customer smart questions. The better your questions the more directed your sales approach can be and, as a result, the more you will sell. Also, smart questions are more useful than small talk which really only wastes time.

So what kind of questions should you ask? It's difficult to be specific as it depends on what you are selling. However, while I can't tell you exactly what to ask, I can tell you what information you need to find out.

1. What exactly does the customer need the product or service for?
2. Have they used something similar before?
3. How quickly do they need it?
4. Do they have a budget in mind?
5. What are their concerns if any?

If you ask the above questions you will learn:

1. Why the customer wants to buy the product or service.
2. Whether they have made a similar purchase before and what their experience of that was.
3. How urgent it is for them to get it, which helps you to sell it quickly.
4. If you can meet their budget.
5. What their issues and concerns are and if you will be able to talk them through these and put their fears to rest.

In my early sales days I used to write my questions in my notebook so that if I froze up at the beginning of a face-to-face meeting I could refer to the list—in as subtle a way as possible. I have also used a questionnaire system very effectively.

I prepare a questionnaire with my questions on it and then fill it in at the meeting. Customers like it and it provides an accurate record. I suggest this method for anyone who struggles with the initial question-asking stage.

Now, I have mentioned many times that being an exceptional listener is a key skill for exceptional sales people. Please remember if you are going to ask a question (and I hope you ask lots), listen carefully to the answers. Be 100 per cent present and involved in the conversation.

#45 Tailor your sales pitch to suit your customers' needs

Many sales people make the huge mistake of blurting out their sales pitch regardless of what the customer is saying. The whole reason for asking questions and becoming a better observer is so you can tailor your presentation to suit the needs of the potential customer.

Let me use an example from the days when I was selling cruises to the Great Barrier Reef to wholesale travel booking firms around the world. My first question to the wholesalers would be about their customers, the people who would be booking the cruises. I would say to each wholesaler: 'Can you tell me a bit about your customers, their age group, their interests and so on?'

Wholesaler #1 responded, 'Our customers are all at least sixty, they are not very active or mobile and the quality of lunch is very important to them.' Based on this answer my presentation went something like this:

> Our cruises are perfect for your market. We pick your customers up in our luxury coaches around 8 a.m. We serve morning tea as soon as they get on board and the boats are big, very comfortable and easy to move around on. We cruise gently out to the Great Barrier Reef, where we have all types of coral viewing vessels so that our customers can see the reef up close without even getting wet. We serve a huge seafood buffet lunch with mountains of prawns, salads, cold meats and hot dishes. Then it's time for the beautiful cruise home and we will have your people back at their hotel by 5.30 p.m., in time for an early dinner.

In answer to the same question, wholesaler #2 said, 'Our customers are party animals. They are 18 to 35, they travel in groups, they are really active and they love to have a great time.' Based on this response my presentation, for exactly the same cruise, went something like this:

> Our cruises are perfect for your market. As soon as we get your customers on board the boat the bar is open. Mind you we have plenty of strong coffee for those people who need a caffeine hit. On the way to the Great Barrier Reef there are plenty of sunbaking lounges and our crew will come around and show them all of the things that can be done while at the reef. We have everything from helicopter scenic flights, scuba diving, snorkelling tours, submarine rides, underwater theatres and heaps more. There is so much to do in the three hours at the reef that I guarantee your customers will have a ball. The bar is open on the way home and we have a guitar player to get the party started. We arrive back in Cairns just as the Blues Bar next to the wharf opens.

Although I was selling the exact same cruise, I tailored my presentation to the individual wholesaler's needs, basing it on the information they gave me. Does this process work? Absolutely! Have a number of variations of your sales pitch ready in your head and pull out the appropriate one based on what the customer tells you.

#46 Beware the robot syndrome

Every sales person has to be wary of falling into the robot syndrome. This is where we stop thinking and just press play when we get into a selling situation. I talk about this in Section 6, Selling over the phone, where telemarketers simply read from a prepared script. It is really irritating to say the least. But when the sales person becomes a robot in a face-to-face situation it becomes downright rude.

There is no doubt that when you are selling the same thing day in and day out it is hard not to say the same things over and over. The information we have to impart is generally going to be the same, but the key here is how you say it. The tone you use, the body language, the eye contact, the energy and the enthusiasm you display all affect the result. Challenge yourself to treat every single interaction as the only one that matters. Pinch yourself when you start to operate on autopilot. Stop and ask the customer a question. Move your body, smile, and animate your voice. Do things that are personal and show that you are totally present for the customer.

Think about this the next time you find a sales person turning into a robot in front of you. See how distracted they are. Look at checkout staff when they ask for your credit card. Notice how their gaze starts to wander while they wait for the machine to do what it does. This time could actually be used to interact with the customer and to make the sales experience that little bit better.

#47 Clarify where to from here

If you are in a position where you have to follow up with the customer it makes sense to clarify what you have to do next. There can often be confusion in a busy shop or on the phone or even in a meeting. I also think we tend to remember only certain parts of an interaction and often what we think we need to do and what the customer is expecting from us don't match.

I like to make this the final part of any interaction. I say exactly what I will be getting back to the customer with, for example a price, a brochure, some technical information and so on. Then I say exactly when I will be getting that information to them. If for some reason I can't get them the information by the time promised I contact them immediately to let them know. This sounds so simple, yet very few sales people ever do it. Clarifying what you will do next will increase your sales conversions dramatically and all it takes is some organisation and communication.

Maybe what you have to do next depends on the customer contacting you. If so, try to get a specific time frame from them and ask if it is okay for you to call them in case they get sidetracked or busy and don't get back to you. This can be done in a very nice way, but it gives you permission to contact them. Always have a second interaction planned.

Another small point, which can make a big difference, is to ensure you have the correct contact details and find out whether they want you to call them, email them, fax them or post information to them. If you cover all bases here it shows you are professional. In a face-to-face meeting checking these details is the logical place to finish a sale for the time being and leaves both parties with a sense of anticipation. (The art of following up is discussed in greater detail in Section 8.)

#48 Always have something to leave behind

I always make a point of leaving something behind after every sales meeting, whether it be a brochure, a product sample, a DVD or even a gift such as a box of chocolates. I want to be remembered. I want the customer to have something on their desk that will make them think of me and what I said, long after our meeting has concluded.

A few years ago I encountered an interesting salesman who sold insurance. His trademark was a business card as big as a greeting card. On the front was a magnificent picture of a small Indian child on the streets of Mumbai with a huge smile on her little face and a message that said something like 'our actions today can change the world tomorrow'. I am still not sure what this had to do with insurance but I couldn't bring myself to throw the card away, it was too big for my card filing system, so I put it on my noticeboard and still read it most days.

Now how is that for a subliminal message? This simple yet very clever concept worked on me. I ended up buying insurance from the man, and I have no doubt that it was because of his card.

Most people are incredibly busy these days. If you are forgotten as soon as you leave the room, your sales job gets a whole lot harder. Spend the money on great promotional material and don't be afraid to give it to people. Make it something you will be remembered by. And be different—stand out from the crowd any way you can.

#49 Write notes to help you remember your customer

When you are in sales you tend to meet a lot of people and collect a lot of business cards. You can end up with a big list of customers and over time it is impossible to remember them all. In my early sales days I would meet literally thousands of new people every year. I collected mounds of business cards and I could never really remember the person on the card. So I started a process that has served me very well for over twenty years.

As soon as I finished a face-to-face meeting I would write some notes on the back of the person's business card. Of course it is a little rude to do this while you are in the meeting and in some cultures it is a big faux pas, so I suggest getting into the habit of doing it in your car or in a coffee shop immediately after the meeting. I write little memory joggers that help me to remember the person afterwards. Sometimes it might be something the person was wearing—'Bill had a Donald Duck tie on.' Or it might be something we spoke about—'Bill used to be a mad keen waterskiier.' Or something to do with the office—'Signed picture of Bill with Madonna on the wall.' These memory joggers still work for me after all these years. If you want to get really smart, keep an index system on your computer or even a manual card system. Both are simply extensions of the same idea and they will be just as effective.

How does this help you become a better sales person? It helps you build relationships. It makes having a conversation easier even if you haven't seen someone for a few years. People are impressed when you remember something about them.

Selling in the long term is all about building relationships. The better you are at achieving this the better you will be at selling anything. We all know that wonderful experience of feeling very important when you go into a coffee shop, bar or restaurant and the sales person remembers what you like to eat or drink. They may not remember your name but they remember other personal details about you.

Take a few moments to write down memory joggers immediately after your meetings and you will enjoy the benefits for years.

Action plan — What can I do right now to become the very best sales person I can be?

*'Knowing is not enough; we must apply.
Willing is not enough; we must do.'*
Johann Wolfgang von Goethe

6 | Selling over the phone

There are various ways that you can sell over the telephone. You might make a cold call. You might call an existing customer who you communicate with often. Or someone might call you to enquire about a product or service that you offer.

In my view, selling over the phone is an art. I employed telemarketers once to sell memberships to a restaurant club and I was constantly amazed at how good they were at talking to complete strangers. They had the right approach to manage the process. Personally, I don't like cold calling prospective customers but over the years I have learnt to do it—I simply apply the same skills that I use to sell in any other situation and it has worked very well. A great sales person can adapt and learn and apply their skills to any selling environment.

This section will help anyone who has to sell products or services over the phone.

\# 50 Start at the beginning
\# 51 Be prepared and have everything in front of you
\# 52 Get your head right before you pick up the phone
\# 53 Apply the same principles as for face-to-face selling
\# 54 It is a numbers game, but quality always outperforms quantity
\# 55 Leave clever, creative messages

#50 Start at the beginning

Sounds logical doesn't it? But where is the beginning? Well, before you can even think about selling over the phone, you need to learn how to talk on the phone or, more significantly, how to be heard on the phone.

Really bad telemarketers have the following attributes:

1. They don't talk clearly so you can't understand what they are saying.
2. They have strong accents, again making it difficult to understand them.
3. They work in environments with lots of background noise.
4. They don't get to the point, but rather waste your time with inane questions like 'How is your day?'
5. They don't ask if they have reached you at a good time, leaping instead into a long-winded, parrot-like script with no gaps where you could stop them.
6. When you finally do get to say something, they don't listen to your answers, but forge on with the script, hoping to wear you down.
7. When you finally say the product isn't really for you, they hang up.

Telemarketing is an old sales technique. Countless books have been written about it and countless training programs developed around the concept, and most seem hell-bent on treating the customer like an idiot. Push the sale through, don't take no for an answer, overcome every objection. We've all been sold something that at the start of the conversation we didn't want. We end up with a really hollow feeling in our belly that is the result of being pressured into buying something. That, to me, is not a good sale.

Avoid the bad habits listed above and develop your own

style. The world has changed; consumers have changed. Be open, be honest and be respectful of the person on the other end of the line. Learn how to talk clearly, make sure you have a quiet work space so that there are no distractions, be clear about what you are selling or promoting and make sure you have reached the person at a convenient time. If you say it will only take a couple of minutes make sure it does.

I know that many sales trainers who specialise in telemarketing would disagree with this, but I believe an honest and forthright approach will produce far greater and far more professional sales in the long run.

#51 Be prepared and have everything in front of you

From my visits to call centres I have noticed that there are three types of people working there.

The first have very sparse, uncluttered work stations. There is usually not much more than a computer terminal and a note pad on their desk, with perhaps a few supporting bits and pieces of information neatly and strategically positioned. They seem to have the answers to any questions firmly locked in their head and they appear in control and organised.

The second type seems to be living in their cubicle, and in some instances it appears that their entire family has moved in with them. Every square centimetre is laden with food and drink, family photos, lists, motivational messages, folders and steadily growing piles of paper. They seem to be completely disorganised but, surprisingly, they generally know exactly where everything is and they can answer any question or find the answer to something in the blink of an eye.

The third type may create a physical environment like either of the above but, whether they operate in a mess or in a Zen-like compartment, they never seem to be able to find anything or answer any question. They always seem to be looking for the magical answer sheet, or piece of paper, or pen. To the person on the other end of the phone this sends a very clear message and it certainly erodes confidence. If you can't even find a pen will your company be able to manage my telecommunications needs?

When selling over the phone, you must make sure that you have a system that works for you. Cluttered or sparse, or somewhere in between, it's up to you. I encourage people to work in an environment that suits them the best. Personalise your space, make it warm, make it inviting and most importantly make it yours. But before you start work on the phone, run through a checklist to make sure you have every single thing you will need to appear calm, confident and organised to your potential customers. This checklist may contain some or all of the following:

1. Plenty of pens and paper.
2. Price lists.
3. Copies of brochures.
4. Technical information files.
5. Copies of advertisements if the customer is likely to be ringing in response to an advertisement.
6. Key selling points of your product or service on a list somewhere easy to see.
7. Additional contact information such as phone numbers, domain names for any website that you may have to refer the customer to, etc.
8. Water—in case you get a tickle in your throat while talking.
9. Tissues—in case you sneeze or need to blow your nose.
10. Plenty of copies of any forms that need to be filled in.

It may sound obvious but next time someone calls you or you call them with a sales enquiry, note how organised they are. And see how your buying mood changes when you have someone totally in control and organised as opposed to someone who appears barely able to answer a phone, let alone inspire confidence in whatever they are selling.

As the boy scout motto goes: be prepared. An exceptional sales person is always prepared.

#52 Get your head right before you pick up the phone

It is important to adopt the right attitude before dialling the number. Some great sales people that I have worked with have little rituals that they perform so they can approach each call in the right frame of mind. The rituals vary, but the outcomes are the same. Generally they stop and take a moment after each call. They finish that call in their head, do any follow-up that needs to be done, then focus on the next call. They think about what they are going to say and the outcome they want to achieve. They reorganise their work station and, when all is in order, they make the call.

Now this may seem like a tortuous approach but it all happens quite quickly. The more you do it, the quicker you get at this 'mind clearing' process. All selling is about attitude. The better the attitude the better the result—simple as that.

People can be rude over the phone. They can be angry, they can be abrupt and they can get quite personal. It's much easier to be like this when you don't have someone sitting in front of you. That's why people selling over the phone need to be able to bounce back from bad experiences quickly, otherwise they can easily become emotional basket cases.

If you have a really bad call, one that rattles you, it might be appropriate to get up and go for a walk. Find something positive, have a laugh or get something to eat or drink to change your emotional state. Likewise when you have a great call, and you are feeling fantastic, keep calling as your mood will really help you to sell more effectively.

In between all calls, stop, take a big breath, clear your head, get prepared and then dial. It might be a bit slower at first but you will soon learn to go through this process in seconds and the results will be noticeable.

#53 Apply the same principles as for face-to-face selling

I think we are on the verge of seeing a resurgence in telemarketing due to increased fuel prices and reduced telecommunication costs. It is much cheaper to have a telemarketer in the office than it is to have a rep on the road. For the same reason I believe we will be seeing more people working from home doing telemarketing. There will be many people working in mainstream sales positions who will be asked to change and become telemarketers. Some will make it, many won't, especially if they don't bring the right attitude to the job.

I have a friend who suddenly went from being a very successful sales rep on the road to a telemarketer. He now sells computer software by phone. He never leaves his house or meets his customers face to face so, if he wanted to, he could make his calls in the nude. Instead, Terry gets up every morning, showers and shaves, puts on a freshly ironed shirt and a tie and goes to 'the office', which is a room off the garage. He sets himself up, checks his email and then starts working. The funniest part of his ritual is that he kisses his wife goodbye and even takes his lunch with him.

Okay, this may seem a little odd but it works for Terry. He sells an amazing amount of software, he is a complete professional and he takes his job seriously. When he first moved to working from home Terry thought it would be great—he could dress in jeans and an old shirt, he wouldn't have to shave every morning, he could play with the kids and sit down and have lunch with his wife every day. But when he did all this, his sales dropped dramatically. He couldn't get into the right zone. He never really felt like he was at work and it showed. For Terry what worked best was to take all the procedures and skills he used in the office and when he was face to face with his customers and apply these to his home office and his new phone clients. This meant that he needed structure and organisation. He also had to learn to research his customers online instead of in the field. He had to learn to develop relationships over the phone. He achieved all of this and he continues to be an amazingly successful sales person.

I guess the key here is to do what works for you. But all too often telesales and mainstream sales are treated as two different worlds. For me, they are the same. If you have the right grounding in face-to-face sales, you can take these skills into the world of telemarketing or telesales.

#54 It is a numbers game, but quality always outperforms quantity

There is no doubt that telemarketing is a numbers game—the more people you talk to the more sales you will tend to make. Hence the obsession at most call centres for telemarketers to make more calls. That said, I believe the world of telemarketing (and sales overall) is changing dramatically. This attitude of treating people like numbers and churning through prospective targets until you get someone compliant enough to sell something to is ending and thank goodness for that.

It is far more important to improve the quality of your approach. Bring honesty, integrity, passion and all those other characteristics we discussed in Section 1 to your selling. Who really wants to be a dodgy sales person? No one reading this book, I imagine. It's more often fly-by-night, high pressure, low quality, ethically challenged businesses that seem to be obsessed with chasing the numbers.

I recommend slowing the process down and making better calls. Focus on having high quality interactions with the prospective customer. This means being sincere with your questions, being upfront about how long you need and, most importantly, getting to the point about how you can assist the customer. The result will be much more uplifting and rewarding for both parties. Treat people as people not as numbers on a list. If you do, your potential customers will pick up on this, with surprisingly positive results.

#55 Leave clever, creative messages

Most telemarketers don't leave messages. They believe that prospective customers won't ring back and most of the time they are right. Why? Because telemarketers tend to leave very uninspired messages that are guaranteed not to get people to call back.

Be a little more creative with the messages that you leave. Be mysterious, be fun, be enticing and, most of all, give the potential customer a reason to call you back. Here are two examples that worked particularly well on me.

I came home to this message on my answering machine:

> Hello Mr Griffiths, it's Harry Smith here from Amazonia restaurant. I notice that you dine here quite often with clients. I imagine you would like to save some money. I can make it so that whenever you dine or entertain you get a 50 per cent discount on your bill. I assume this would be appealing so can you give me a call back when you have a moment? It will only take a few minutes to organise. Thanks very much for your business and your time. My number is . . .

I rang back immediately. I found out that Harry was selling a loyalty card that would cost $200 a year and save me 50 per cent on my food and beverage bills whenever I dined at this restaurant or at many others in the same network around the world. Did I buy it? Of course.

Countless hotel loyalty program telemarketers have tracked me down and tried to sell me similar products. I never had an overwhelming desire to call them back because I never really believed in what they were trying to sell me.

This chap was very smart, very effective. He told me that he made 90 per cent of his sales from leaving messages and that, in fact, he preferred to leave messages because he knew that if someone rang back they were already interested, they were ringing at a time convenient for them and even though they didn't necessarily know what the product was they were halfway there because they already wanted the saving.

Harry's was a very clever, simple and unorthodox approach to telemarketing. In my mind, the way of the future. Here is another example of an effective message left on my machine:

> Hello Mr Griffiths, Jennifer Aitken here. I have just spoken to one of your neighbours and I managed to save them $1000 a year on their phone bill, in about three minutes. I thought you might be interested in hearing about the same opportunity. If you are, please give me a call. I am sure it will be the easiest and fastest $1000 you will make and don't we all need that? My number is . . .

Again this message is creative and clever. Jennifer developed credibility by mentioning one of my neighbours (which could be anyone in the city of course), she got my attention by talking about a large saving that would only take a couple of minutes to sort out, and then she connected with me by saying how we all want and need to save money. Did I ring her back? Absolutely.

So don't get hung up about answering machines or message bank. Get creative, think about your message and make the answering machine your new best friend. Come up with a message that people have to respond to because it is so enticing and powerful.

Action plan — What can I do right now to become the very best sales person I can be?

SELLING OVER THE PHONE

'The law of cause and effect: If you do what other successful people do, you will eventually get the results that other successful people get.'

Brian Tracy

7 | The challenge of the internet

It wasn't that long ago that there was no such thing as the internet, yet today it is hard to imagine life without it. To the world of sales it has brought many new challenges and new opportunities. The internet is spectacularly amazing in every way. It provides an enormous platform to reach the world, to sell anything to anyone and to allow one sales person at home in their pyjamas to seem like a big company. It is limited only by our own imagination and it is the perfect forum in which to be creative, to rethink the old ways of selling and to do it better.

I believe that most of the tried and tested sales skills are just as important online as they are in the more traditional sales arenas. But for some reason, a lot of the fundamentals of selling seem to have fallen by the wayside.

In this section we will look how to sell in the technological age.

56 Where do businesses go wrong when selling on the internet?
57 The old principles still apply
58 Before you press 'send', stop and think
59 Embrace change—it's not so scary
60 Use viral marketing
61 You have only a few seconds to engage and compel

#56 Where do businesses go wrong when selling on the internet?

Overall, businesses are becoming more sophisticated when it comes to using the internet. Websites are loading faster, graphics are getting much clearer and more visually creative, wider bandwidths means more video footage is being used and we are able to take advantage of larger downloads resulting in more online interaction with our customers. However, despite all these improvements, it is surprising how many businesses still get it wrong when it comes to selling online.

Here are some of the most common errors I come across:

1. The website contains a mass of information but it is confusing, it is designed in no logical manner and the customer has to play detective to buy anything.
2. Endless forms have to be filled in, only to fail when we press the submit button, requiring us to start all over again.
3. Links don't work, making it impossible to buy anything.
4. Ridiculous policies and procedures are included, all designed for the seller's benefit but of little or no value to the customer.
5. Copy is poorly written.
6. Long, unique log-in passwords that can't be changed to suit the user have to be recalled.

The list goes on. We have all experienced the frustration of using websites that don't work well. The golden rule is to make it as easy as possible for customers to buy from us online. Spend some time looking at websites that sell really well. What do they do differently from the really complicated ones? I find Amazon.com to be one of the easiest sites to buy products from, and clearly so do tens of millions of other people. Another impressive site is Wotif.com, a last-minute hotel-

THE CHALLENGE OF THE INTERNET

booking business that I use a lot. It is very easy to find what you want, the prices are good and making a booking takes less than a minute.

You don't need a big budget to make a great, customer-friendly website that encourages people to buy from you. What you do need is a desire to look at your site with fresh eyes, applied logic and a good dose of creativity. The last step is to make everything as simple as possible. Do this and you can't help but win online.

#57 The old principles still apply

There are a number of important principles that should always be adhered to regardless of the sales environment you are operating in. Without a doubt the absolute priority for any online business should be a quick response. How many times do you visit a website and make an enquiry, only to have to wait for days for a response, if you get one at all?

One example that really drives this home (excuse the pun) is a group of car hire companies that advertise on a web portal site. Potential customers visit the site and email all the businesses to check rates, availability, etc. Each of the twelve similar companies has the same size advertisement and their rates do not vary greatly. But one company gets 90 per cent of the business from the site and it has nothing to do with their advertisement. They have a policy of responding to enquiries within two hours; they have employed people to monitor emails twenty-four hours a day. The other companies respond when they get around to it, if at all.

The online environment is much less formal than the face-to-face one. Sales people tend to be more informal. Emails are often poorly written, with names spelt incorrectly, titles not used and responses generally short, leaving customers needing more information. It is hard to check up on the staff—whether they are responding immediately, who is setting the standard in terms of the quality of responses, what information is being sent and so on.

I believe it is absolutely essential to treat customers (both existing and potential) with total respect, and this applies in all sales environments. I see this as an amazing opportunity simply because many businesses are so poor in this area.

Adopt the exact same principles online as you would in any other selling situation and you will see extraordinary results because you will stand out from the crowd.

#58 Before you press 'send', stop and think

One of the problems with modern communication is that it is very fast. We act and react quickly to messages that we receive and while this is very convenient, sometimes we miss opportunities.

It is easy to get into the habit of 'blurting out' email messages; we type at the speed of light and then press send without looking at what we have written. There is a lot to be gained by taking a moment to review what we have typed and to ask a few simple questions:

1. Have I been respectful in my email?
2. Have I been clear and to the point?
3. Have I explained everything as best as I can?
4. Have I made it clear what I will be doing from here and what, if anything, I need the customer to do?
5. Have I been friendly and engaging without being overly familiar?
6. Have I been as professional as I want to be?

Taking a few moments to consider your correspondence is a smart thing to do. For most of us, the act of sitting down and writing a letter is a dim memory from the past. In the digital world we type, correct (sometimes) and send. When you write a letter, it is a whole different ball game, and by 'write' I mean use a pen and paper. If you want to get your message across in a clear and effective manner, you have to think carefully before you write as fixing mistakes is messy. And you have to think about the spelling of words because you are the only spell check program available. Try it and see just how much thought you put into writing a letter as opposed to blurting out an email.

Producing carefully considered communication is yet another way to stand out from the crowd. It is a way to build rapport, to show respect and to impress potential and existing customers with your level of professionalism.

Give it a go. Follow this simple three-step plan when writing emails—STOP, CONSIDER, SEND.

#59 Embrace change—it's not so scary

We live in a world that is changing at a ridiculously rapid rate. Some people struggle with this rate of change but, like it or not, it is certainly going to continue. It makes much more sense to embrace change rather than resist it.

From my experience, change generally brings opportunities, even though at first we may not recognise them. Today there are many new ways to communicate and these all provide new selling opportunities. To succeed we need to learn how to use these new communication platforms so we can sell to all markets instead of approaching everyone in the same way. How we should sell to a twenty-year-old, for example, is totally different from how we sell to a sixty-year-old. Many businesses struggle with these new methods of communication and revert to doing what they know best: using one approach for all. This used to work, but it certainly doesn't now.

To understand and make use of the new online communities and the power of email as a sales tool we need to invest in educating ourselves and our staff. We need to change what we say and how we say it. When I realised I needed to know more about the online world, specifically the markets I didn't understand, I employed a twenty-one-year-old university graduate to educate me. I asked him to do a review of online communities—who they were, how to communicate with them, how to sell to them and so on. The report he compiled amazed me. Reading it was like learning a new language or discovering a new planet. Of course this probably says more about me than about anyone else but I felt like I had been living with my head in the sand for the last few years.

Once I started to learn more about this new world, it certainly became less scary and I started to discover amazing opportunities there. I now make the effort to spend time researching the new online environments. I explore online communities like MySpace and Facebook, eBay, YouTube, various blogs and any other communication forums I can find. I look for ways to apply what I know to these new environments and I come across exceptional opportunities at every turn.

It is significant that Hillary Clinton chose to launch her campaign for president of the United States on YouTube. This was previously unheard of and it shows just how important these new ways of communicating are to the world.

#60 Use viral marketing

While not the nicest of names, viral marketing is just the new term for word-of-mouth marketing and it is generally applied to the online world. The best example of viral marketing and how it works is YouTube. This business started pretty small, as a place for people to easily post their own videos online. It was convenient and cost effective as a storage system. Then people started sharing their favourite YouTube clips with others and in a short period of time, tens of millions of people were watching a huge range of online videos, rantings and promotions. Today, presidential candidates start their campaigns on YouTube, new products are launched daily on YouTube, bands launch their latest clips on YouTube, and so on. Viral marketing is very powerful.

I recently met a young entrepreneur who specialises in arranging special events, open to the public, where people come and listen to various presenters talking on all types of subjects from financial planning to personal development. Over the space of a year Daniel and his team get thousands of people to attend these events and buy his products and services, simply by applying viral marketing to his network.

To make viral marketing work you need to become exceptional at collecting email addresses. Email addresses can be collected from many sources. The more the merrier but they need to be great quality contacts. Be warned, though—in many countries sending unsolicited emails is illegal (not that you would think so considering how much spam we all get). I suggest working with your web developer to come up with the best ideas and methods to collect email addresses and send out information in a legal manner.

There are a lot of businesses that have cut their advertising budget down to virtually nothing simply because they have become very good at viral marketing. They put their time and energy into building quality databases and they produce smart, visually impressive and creative email information that people want to receive and that encourages them to buy.

Every day I have some experience that reinforces to me the value and importance of selling online. It is a vibrant, constantly evolving environment that is only limited by your own imagination and the ability of the people building your site (well, perhaps your budget as well). To succeed in this arena you must have an open mind to the potential that the internet provides for virtually any business. Be prepared to try new ideas, change what doesn't work and look for ideas on other sites that are working well and you will be halfway there.

#61 You have only a few seconds to engage and compel

I spend a lot of time researching websites. I don't necessarily care what they are selling—I am far more interested in how they sell, how they promote themselves, how they communicate and how they compel me to buy from them. If you are serious about using the internet to sell your products or services, I suggest you do the same. We need to open our minds to the possibilities the internet provides. Too many businesses simply put their brochure online when they have the chance to do so much more.

There is no such thing as convention when it comes to the online world. Every time you type in a URL address or click on a link you feel expectant. What will this website be like? Will it be impressive or hopeless? Will I find what I am looking for? Will I get frustrated? Will I be impressed?

The first few seconds after arriving at a website are no different from the first few seconds after meeting someone face to face. We form a host of opinions, right or wrong, about the site and the business it represents. This is why I never understand why some businesses (and large corporations) have such terrible websites. Websites need to draw the customers in. They need to engage and connect with the people they are targeted at, and follow a logical progression that works for these customers. I am not saying your website needs bells and whistles, but certainly it needs to make a powerful impression in those first few seconds or it will lose them.

Put that extra thought into how you can make your website both engaging and compelling from the start and your sales will increase immediately.

Action plan — What can I do right now to become the very best sales person I can be?

THE CHALLENGE OF THE INTERNET

'You don't have to be great to get started, but you have to get started to be great.'
Les Brown

8 | The art of following up

I do a lot of work for a company called Enhance Plus which monitors customer satisfaction. They are engaged by companies to contact customers directly to gather feedback on the level of service and overall degree of satisfaction being experienced. They talk to people who have been given a quote but haven't yet purchased, to people who have just made a purchase and to long-term customers who have relationships with that company going back many years. Enhance Plus makes thousands of calls each month, representing businesses across virtually every industry sector imaginable.

The main issue they encounter consistently is a lack of follow-up by the business or specifically by the individual sales person. There are lots of promises but very little action. If you master the art of following up, you will be miles ahead of the rest of the pack and your sales will grow because you have happy, satisfied customers who provide word-of-mouth referrals.

In this section I am going to share some very simple techniques that will help you to become a 'follow-up guru'.

\# 62 Clarify what the customer is expecting from you
\# 63 Ask the customer when they want you to contact them
\# 64 Great follow-up takes great organisation
\# 65 Under promise and over deliver—always

101 WAYS TO SELL MORE OF ANYTHING TO ANYONE

\# 66 Don't send boring follow-up letters
\# 67 Never assume—always check that the customer received what you sent

#62 Clarify what the customer is expecting from you

The end of a sales interaction is often a bit of a blur. Lots of things are happening, people are getting ready to leave, your mind begins to wander to what's ahead. I think this often leads to some last-minute mix-ups which can bring the whole sales process undone. We can forget what we have promised to do, like sending more information, and then we wonder why we never hear from that customer again.

I have trained myself to always spend the last few minutes of any meeting clarifying who will do what from here. I make a point of ensuring that everyone in the meeting is focused and that we are all 100 per cent clear on what the next course of action will be, whether it is something I have to do or the customer. I ensure that the customer is totally happy with the course of action we have discussed and I give them very specific details regarding when the follow-up will occur.

This habit has eliminated the grey areas for me—I leave a meeting knowing exactly where I stand and I believe my customers do as well. This is not only professional, it is courteous.

Never assume, always clarify—this is my motto for every meeting I have.

#63 Ask the customer when they want you to contact them

This is another very simple tip but one that is amazingly powerful. Some sales people do it well, others feel that it is a little pushy. I like it and use it all the time. As I have mentioned elsewhere, it is important to communicate on the customer's terms.

Now I don't tend to ask an open-ended question. I always make a suggestion regarding time frames. For example, I say something like: 'I am sure you will need a few days to think this through and to make a decision. Shall I call you next Tuesday at this time?'

This achieves a number of things. It shows respect for the customer by giving them time to think. It takes the immediate pressure off them. It demonstrates your professionalism—you are organised enough to book them in for a follow-up call a week in advance. It gives a clear deadline for the decision-making process. And, most importantly, it shows that this is going to be a relationship, not just a one-off interaction.

#64 Great follow-up takes great organisation

It is really hard to be a follow-up guru if you don't keep good records or if you are not organised. I believe this is an area where a lot of sales people fall down and a lot of sales are lost.

There really is no excuse for not being organised, but some people are better at it than others. I think the key is to make sure that you have a system that works for you. There are plenty of books and courses on getting organised and the ones I have seen are all pretty good, however it is a very personal thing.

I know people who have a totally clear desk but can't seem to find anything. They lose people's names or phone numbers, are always late, and sometimes they miss appointments altogether. Most of the time they couldn't be relied upon to find their way out of a wet paper bag. And then there are people whose work space is an absolute junkyard. Despite the clutter and piles of mess, they know exactly where everything is. They are extremely organised and they are on top of everything that needs to be done. What does this mean?

There is no simple answer here. You simply have to work out a system that suits you. What I do know is that you need to be able to keep track of your customers, you need a good diary system that is updated daily, and you need to be disciplined enough to write down all future follow-up requirements and make sure you do them.

If you really do struggle to be organised, try to find a friend in the sales field who has similar responsibilities and see what system they use. It is a trial and error situation. Some people like electronic diaries, other people still work on paper. Personally I like a combination of the two.

#65 Under promise and over deliver — always

Disappointment seems to be a common topic when people talk about their most recent purchases. I was speaking to a friend recently who is trying to get a house built. It is a big house, on a fantastic block, but he has been to eleven builders so far and not a sod of soil has been turned. The problem is that the builders are all busy. They make promises to deliver plans and quotes by a certain time but they constantly fail to deliver. Clearly this is frustrating and I am sure my friend is not the only person in the world to be experiencing this at the moment.

There are ways to turn disappointment around and to convert more sales simply by changing your customers' expectations, which is where the whole problem begins. If a sales person says they will have a quote to us by 5 p.m. that day, we expect to see that quote by 5 p.m. The real problem is that as sales people we often feel pressured to deliver within an unrealistic time frame even though we know it will be impossible to do so.

My advice is very simple. No matter how hard you are pushed by your customer, overestimate the time it will take you to deliver. For example, if you know you could get your quote to them by midday the next day, tell them you will get it to them by 5 p.m. Tell them that you will move heaven and earth to get it to them sooner but it is unlikely. When you get it to them by midday, you will have exceeded their expectations already.

Our aim should always be to under promise and over deliver. If you do this you will convert more sales and develop a fan base of customers who tell everyone that you are amazing. It really is that simple. Of course we should do the same with every part of our business. The more we are pressured into responding to unrealistic time frames or ridiculous prices, the more likely we are to fail to meet the customers' expectations.

Under promise and over deliver a few times and you will see just how powerful a strategy it is. You will wonder why you didn't use it long ago.

#66 Don't send boring follow-up letters

If you are going to send a follow-up letter, which I recommend you do, whether it be after a sales presentation or after a purchase, make it a memorable one. Don't fall into the common trap of writing a standard boring letter that is nice but really doesn't do a great deal. Get creative with your follow-up letter. Be unexpected and be extraordinary. Several years ago I booked a holiday to India. I was very excited about the trip as my books had just been published there and I was going to meet the Indian publishers. I booked through my local travel agent. It was a little complicated but my consultant did a great job and managed to avoid showing any irritation when I changed my schedule a hundred times.

A few weeks after I booked the trip I got a package in the mail from my travel agent. It was filled with information about India. Not travel brochures, but more factual stuff: maps, travel guides and photocopied articles from magazines. It was such a surprise and a delight. I read it all and enjoyed every moment while thinking wonderful thoughts about my travel agent.

I think we can all devise some pretty amazing follow-up actions if only we take the time to think about it. After I do a keynote presentation I send my client a framed copy of one of my books. Sure, it costs me a few hundred dollars to frame the book and ship it, but it is unexpected and that is why I do it. Next time you are sitting down to write your standard follow-up letter, why not throw it out the window and come up with an extraordinary letter or gift that will get your customers shouting to the world about you?

#67 Never assume—always check that the customer received what you sent

It is amazing how often other people can mess up the follow-up process. For example, let's say you meet a customer, promise to send them a catalogue, make a note for your assistant to send it, then sit back and wait for the customer to call you to place an order. Nothing happens. After a few weeks you finally call them, only to discover they never received the catalogue. When you investigate you find out that the catalogues were out of stock but that the people in marketing didn't tell your assistant, who lost track of the request due to all the other things he had to do. The end result? The customer loses faith in you and your business.

I make it a rule *never* to assume that the customer has received what I have sent them. I always make a follow-up call to check. But before I do that I make sure that everything has worked from our end, so if the customer hasn't received the material I can say that it was dispatched by Mary at 5 p.m. last Friday by Express Post to this address.

It is both surprising and distressing how many sales people never follow up. I have seen sales people triple their business in a few weeks simply by following up on quotes that they had sent out. They make a quick call to the customer to check that they got the quote and, while they are talking to them, take the opportunity to see if they need any more information or perhaps would like to make an order. Believe it or not, up to 80 per cent of quotes are never followed up. If your business is one of those that lets quotes slip through the cracks, implement a quote follow-up service immediately (in fact you can even outsource this).

Never assume anything in the world of sales. Communication is king and the better you are at it, the more diligent you are and the easier you make it for people to buy from you, the more you will sell of anything.

Action plan — What can I do right now to become the very best sales person I can be?

THE ART OF FOLLOWING UP

'Hope sees the invisible, feels the intangible and achieves the impossible.'
Charles Caleb Cotton

9 | Closing the sale

This is without doubt the most talked about part of the sales process. There are countless books written about closing the sale, there are hundreds of sales courses on this topic, and it is a subject that often gets sales professionals a little hot under the collar.

In simple terms, closing the sale refers to that specific point when the customer either agrees to buy from you or they say no. It is often awkward, there is uncertainty and in many ways it is like a first kiss — we never know how to do it well, or where it will lead, but it feels kind of nice.

In this section I will share with you a few of my best recommendations to help you close more sales.

68 Learn to read the signals that someone is ready to buy
69 Be brave enough to ask for the business
70 Act like the sale is a foregone conclusion
71 Objections are not always bad
72 Have a win/win philosophy
73 If it's not going well, get to the real problem
74 Keep a surprise or two up your sleeve
75 Very few people are good at closing — make it your mission

#68 Learn to read the signals that someone is ready to buy

As you get more experienced as a sales professional you can start to read the signals that tell you a customer is ready to buy. Knowing what these signals are is half the battle. Of course it can vary depending on the types of products and services that you sell, but here are some of the best ones:

1. The customer asks questions about money, payment options and payment terms.
2. The customer wants to know how soon they could have the item, specifically if they are in stock. They may also ask about delivery for larger items.
3. They lean in towards you and you can often sense a general relaxing of their mood because they have made their decision. I find that the customer often gets playful and laughs, which means that all tension is gone and they are ready to buy.
4. The customer wants to know about the warranty period and your after-sale service.
5. They make clarification statements like 'So the best price is $999. Is that right?' This means they are getting ready to make a decision but it could still go either way.
6. The customer changes the subject. This can mean that they have made a decision and are ready to get on with it. It is important that you stop selling now and start closing.
7. They ask questions about who else has purchased the product or service. They may possibly be looking for a testimonial to reinforce the fact that they are making the right decision.
8. They ask you to repeat some information or details to make sure they are clear before making the final commitment.

9. They ask you for your opinion on the product with questions like: 'Do you think this is the best product for me?'
10. There is a lot of head nodding. This means that the customer likes what you are saying and agrees with you.

You might not get all of these signals but even a couple should encourage you to move towards asking for the business. Over time, reading these signals will become second nature. Be patient and, as mentioned in many sections in this book, the key is to become a keen observer of the people you are selling to.

#69 Be brave enough to ask for the business

This is a really powerful piece of advice for any sales person. The moment when you actually ask the customer for the purchase can sometimes feel awkward for both you and the customer, but you need to overcome this. I struggled with using the term 'brave' but in reality that's what you have to be. It is much easier to give the customer all of the information and then leave them to make a decision, but this is a passive way of selling which produces mediocre results. I remember vividly the first time I asked a customer if they would like to buy the set of scuba gear I had just presented to them. They nodded their head emphatically and it was clear that my question sealed the deal.

You can ask for the sale in a number of ways. You can lead into it by asking for their opinion on what you have just presented, if they need any more information or if they have any concerns. If the answers are consistently positive, make the leap and ask them if they would like to buy these products now.

Like everything to do with sales, I guarantee that this will get easier. Every time you ask, you get one step closer to making it second nature.

#70 Act like the sale is a foregone conclusion

I use this particular sales closing technique because I actually believe it. Why on earth wouldn't the customer want to buy what I am selling? I don't mean to sound arrogant but I really do believe in the services that I sell and promote. Because of this I have absolutely no doubt that I will not only deliver on my promises but will also exceed my customers' expectations in every way. I also believe that if you have done your homework, presented well, responded to any questions with the right answers and the product is what the customer needs, it should be a foregone conclusion.

We all have our own style. Mine is certainly not pushy but it is confident. There is a big difference between the two. I think that this confidence shines through and it puts the customer at ease. Remember, if you are uncertain it shows.

#71 Objections are not always bad

There is a lot of discussion about how to overcome objections. This is when the customer raises questions that suggest they are not interested, or are losing interest, in the sale. But what objections can do is give you an opportunity to allay their fears. Objections can be related to a host of different topics including time frames for supply, pricing, quality, colours, after-sale service, questions about the company to ascertain if it is credible, as well as general uncertainty. Often objections may simply arise because the customer isn't sure if they can afford the product and, of course, this is very reasonable.

I like to think that the objections stage of the sales process is where you earn your money. It is where you can make or break the sale and it is where people sense very clearly if they are not being told the truth. So make sure you have all the answers ready and they need to be good.

I recently did some training for a sales representative from a gelato manufacturing business. The rep was very experienced in the industry but not overly experienced in the world of sales. Sitting down and having an informal conversation with him revealed his amazing knowledge. But when he was put in front of potential wholesale customers he got very nervous and did little to impress them. This was very frustrating both for him and for the company that employed him.

So we made up a list of every possible question or objection that could be asked or made by potential customers, and I mean everything. It was a long list. He then provided responses to these questions and objections in our informal conversation mode and we wrote them down.

Then we set about role-playing them all in a more formal mode. In the end I could ask him any question, make any objection and he would have the perfect answer. He has gone on to become a very good sales manager and now it is a role he really enjoys.

This is a great exercise for anyone in sales. I think it should be mandatory. Don't assume that sales staff know how to answer the curly questions because often they don't. They may simply say what they think is right or what the other sales people say, which may be right, but it could easily be wrong.

Write down every possible question or objection, answer them truthfully and then role-play them—even if it is by yourself.

#72 Have a win/win philosophy

I have found that going into every negotiation with a win/win philosophy has really helped me to close a lot of sales. If you have to negotiate your price so low that your business can't make any money out of the sale, why bother? If the price is too high and the customer simply can't afford it, you need to find another option. The key is to find middle ground where both parties win.

There are lots of reasons why people hesitate when it comes time to either make the purchase or not. They may want to buy but they need to talk to their partner, or think through their finances, or really decide if this is what they want. I am not a believer in trying to push people over the line. I think it can backfire on you and leave the customer with buyer's remorse. If you start to back a customer into a corner you may find that they react by taking their business elsewhere and you can't really blame them.

Most sales are a form of negotiation. You want to make the sale and the customer wants to make the purchase. All we need to do is facilitate the transaction to make it happen.

#73 If it's not going well, get to the real problem

Sometimes the whole sales process seems to go belly up. Nothing is working, the customer seems agitated, you feel out of sorts and uncomfortable, and the whole situation seems to be going haywire. You have said everything that you can and you know that there is nothing more to say, so now should be the time to ask for the sale but it just doesn't feel right.

I suggest you stop what you are doing and ask the customer what is really going on. Be honest with them. Tell them that you feel that something is wrong and try to find out what their concerns are. There is no logical reason to keep battling on if the customer is clearly not with you.

It may take some time before you get confident enough to do this, but I am sure you will. This, like many other sales skills, will develop the more often you use it.

#74 Keep a surprise or two up your sleeve

Over the years I have learnt to always hold a surprise or two up my sleeve. These surprises can help to sweeten the deal or to cement the relationship with the customer.

I don't like the bartering method of negotiation, common in many countries. When I ask for a price I want the best price first and that's that. But of course not everyone is the same. Some people really enjoy the bartering process. It makes them feel they have had a win and I think that's fine. For this reason I have learnt to always keep a little room to move on price, quantity, deliverables or other ways to add value.

I also learnt a really nice technique from a friend of mine who sells houses, clearly a high value commodity. He always makes a point of throwing in an extra item after the deal is signed to thank the customers for their business. Now at this stage of the sales process the last thing the customers expect is something for free as they have already done all of the negotiating. That is what makes this such a clever idea.

CLOSING THE SALE

#75 Very few people are good at closing—make it your mission

Yes it's true—very few people are actually good at closing a sale. Most are good at giving all of the information, or building the rapport, but few are actually very good at sealing the deal.

I certainly struggled with the concept early on in my sales career, but when paying the rent depended on it, I soon learnt to get much better at it. I read a lot of books about selling and most had chapter after chapter describing the different kinds of closings. While I have given you some advice about closing, I suggest you read much more. Read as many books on selling as you can. There are many different techniques for closing a sale. Some will suit certain products and services better than others. Try a few different techniques and work out what style suits you. Unfortunately you will have to get it wrong a few times and blow a few sales to figure out what works best for you but it will pay off in the long run.

Observe how other sales people attempt to close you. You will notice that most are terrible at it but every once in a while you will meet someone who is a great closer and you will find yourself pulling out your credit card before you even realise you are doing it.

Some of the best sales closers that I have come across are in the menswear industry. That could of course be because I am an easy person to sell to, but generally menswear sales people are good at all of the key steps and before you know it you are standing in front of a mirror, deciding whether to put the new suit on Visa or Amex.

If you can master the art of closing, you will be in high demand as an employee. If you own a business you will dramatically increase your revenue. Invest in learning this skill, accept that there is some trial and error required, and you will reap big rewards.

Action plan — What can I do right now to become the very best sales person I can be?

CLOSING THE SALE

'Begin somewhere. You can't build a reputation on what you intend to do.'

Liz Smith

10 | It's a marathon, not a sprint

Smart sales people realise that selling is a marathon event. You have to train, you have to be prepared to go the distance and there are bound to be a few hurdles along the way. This section explains the concept of the sales marathon and provides valuable advice to help you become fit enough to go the distance and be the first one across the finish line.

\# 76 Look at the big picture
\# 77 Remember they are *your* customers!
\# 78 Often the most difficult customers become your greatest fans
\# 79 Sometimes you have to walk away
\# 80 Beware of sales burnout
\# 81 What to do when you hit a hurdle

#76 Look at the big picture

Whenever you are involved in selling, it is easy to get sidetracked by focusing only on what is happening right here and now. While I encourage sales people to be focused on being present and in the moment, sales is a long-term proposition and to succeed you really do need to be able to look at the big picture, from many different angles.

For me, looking at the big picture starts with my own business. I think about where I am going, what I want to achieve, and how much revenue I need to reach my goals. I also think about the type of customers I want to attract. I ask myself how I can help their businesses with my products and services, and how I can help them achieve their goals. So I am looking at the big picture for my clients as well and this has been a very successful part of my overall sales strategy, regardless of what I am selling or what my clients are selling. I always take the time to get to know their business, to really understand the key people and what their vision is. The better I know these things the better I can sell to them, the more products and services I can develop with their business in mind and, most importantly, the better our relationship will become.

One of the biggest mistakes made by sales people the world over is a short-term, instant gratification sale. I see it a lot in advertising sales reps. Most are only concerned with making the sale right now. They are often very unconcerned about whether or not the advertisement works. In other words, they have no interest in the big picture for their client. As a result, they wonder why they have little or no client loyalty and why people are often rude and abrupt with them. Clearly not all advertising sales people are like this but I have certainly encountered a lot who are.

As a sales person, the better able you are to look at the big picture in every situation you are faced with, the greater your overall sales results will be.

#77 Remember they are *your* customers!

The people you sell to are *your* customers. Sure, they may be buying from a specific business for any number of reasons, but a true sales professional knows that if they look after their customers, sell to them in a professional manner, provide impeccable service and treat them with total respect, they will keep these customers for a long, long time. This sense of ownership makes smart sales people go the extra mile. It makes them protective of their customers and it makes them do the things that result in long-term relationships, not one-off sales.

An exceptional sales person does whatever it takes to keep their customers happy. There are many ways that the sales person is rewarded for this service and attitude. Their customers are incredibly loyal, they will refer as much business as they can, they will buy new products from the sales person even if there is not a lot of evidence to support the value of the product or service and, last but not least, they will follow the sales person to wherever they are working.

I know that when I sold travel to travel wholesalers, it didn't matter which products I was selling. Those customers who liked me, with whom I had built a strong relationship and had serviced really well, would always buy whatever product I was selling, because they trusted me and believed in me—in other words, they were buying me. This made me attractive to prospective employers because I was able to bring a loyal and extensive customer base with me or, as a bare minimum, access to this customer base.

Treat your customers as your own and treat them as you would like to be treated and not only will they remain loyal to you but you will acquire more new customers than you could ever imagine.

#78 Often the most difficult customers become your greatest fans

I have encountered some real doozies over the years—customers who were so tough and so demanding that I wondered why they even bothered to come and see me. While selling everything from encyclopaedias to commercial diving services, I often came across people for whom everything seemed to be a problem, and when it came to talking money, mamma mia, they were the toughest negotiators imaginable. What I discovered was that everyone who deals with these difficult people finds them challenging, but that most people give up and walk away.

Now, I do believe there is a time to walk away, but as I have said before, patience and persistence do pay off. Some of my toughest customers have become my best customers, though in the beginning I would never have imagined that was possible. I have spoken to sales people from all kinds of industries who agree that some of the most irritating, demanding and downright unpleasant people can grow into the most loyal and committed customers and many even become friends. You simply have to be persistent and let the relationship work. If you keep persisting where others walked away early, these customers will sit up and take notice.

#79 Sometimes you have to walk away

While it is possible to turn a really challenging customer into a fan, there are times when you do have to walk away from people who are too hard to deal with. The trick is to know when to persist and when to walk away.

There are customers that you simply can't please, no matter how hard you try. Every single sale seems to be a concern because deep down you know they will be back to complain about something. You can't win. Accept that you can't keep all of the people happy all of the time and those customers who are simply too hard to deal with, unreasonably demanding, terrible at paying or downright unpleasant need to be cut loose. One of the great things about owning your own business is that you can say adios to those customers whose business is simply not worth having. The same principle has to be applied to a sale. If it is too hard, too soul destroying and too unpleasant, let the customer go and they can drive your competitors crazy. Spend your time looking for new customers who won't be such a chore to work with or to sell to.

I can't really explain how you figure out when a customer is too hard to deal with. I know that I have got much better at following my gut instinct—if it doesn't feel right I do something about it straightaway. This might not work for everyone but those people who have been in business for a while will know exactly what I mean.

#80 Beware of sales burnout

Sales can be very demanding. It doesn't matter whether you are standing behind a cash register all day at the local hardware store or selling planes for Boeing, it is challenging on many levels. Sales people can easily 'burn out' if they are not careful. If you don't have a way to recharge your batteries, to look after your brain and your body, your effectiveness as a sales person will be diminished and that will be reflected in your sales.

What are the key indicators of 'sales burnout'?

1. You start getting grumpy with your customers.
2. You struggle to motivate yourself.
3. Your attention to detail starts to drop.
4. Your sales results are in a downward spiral.
5. You find it hard to source new leads.
6. Your creativity dries up.
7. Your fellow staff members start to bug you.
8. You no longer enjoy selling.

It is important to have a life outside work. If you're not careful, your job can become all consuming. You can end up spending all your time talking about work, talking about selling and talking about customers. It is an easy trap to fall into and it is really boring for anyone who doesn't work in the same job.

I speak from experience. I was a total and absolute workaholic for years. Seven days a week, at least twelve to sixteen hours a day, all I did was work, work, work. I eventually had a bit of a meltdown, some health issues, a great relationship ended because of my obsession and I realised that I had to make some considerable changes to my life. As a result I wrote one of my most successful books, *101 Ways to Have a Business and a Life*, which really addressed the topic of work/life balance.

IT'S A MARATHON, NOT A SPRINT

Make a list of the things you really love doing, things that excite you and fill you with anticipation. Let's call them hobbies. If it has been more than twelve months since you have done any of them they are no longer hobbies, they are memories.

Sales people are attracted to other sales people. In fact there is an old saying that the easiest person to sell to is a sales person, hence they often spend lots of time socialising with each other. I have friends who sell everything from radio advertising to new cars and who often spend their 'down' time socialising with other members of their sales team. While it is great to spend time with the people you work with, once again it is vital you have a life outside of your work arena to help prevent burnout.

Do fun things that rock your boat and you will be a far more effective sales person than if you just work all the time and socialise with the same people that you work with.

#81 What to do when you hit a hurdle

The greatest danger for a sales person is loss of confidence. Anyone who has spent any time selling anything will tell you that from time to time you will hit a hurdle. It might be a really difficult customer, it might be the loss of a big account, or it might be a period where you just can't seem to get a sale. The longer this period goes on the more your confidence can be shaken.

I have experienced many hurdles in the sales world. I know what it feels like to look at the list of people you have to go see that day and feel nothing but dread at the prospect of not making any sales. What can you do?

1. First, accept that you are experiencing a sales slump, not the end of the world. You haven't lost the ability to sell, your career isn't over, your business isn't about to go bust. You are in a rut and it will end.
2. If what you are doing isn't working, change what you are doing. Start at the beginning. Review every stage of your sales system and look for ways to do things differently and perhaps better.
3. Talk to some of your current customers. Try to find out what is going on. Is it you or your business or is it simply that your customers have stopped spending? In other words, find out the facts.
4. Find a mentor—someone who knows and who has been in sales for a long time. Ask for their opinion and advice.
5. Do a training course. Even if you cover the basics of selling again, it will fire you up and reinvigorate you.
6. Have a holiday. If you need a good long break, take one.
7. Do plenty of follow-up calls on your existing customers if this is appropriate and ask them for referrals.
8. Have brainstorming sessions with the other sales people in your business.

IT'S A MARATHON, NOT A SPRINT

9. Get organised. Take the time to get rid of all of those niggling little jobs and projects that are 'incomplete'. Get these sorted and your life will feel much more organised and uncluttered and so will your head.
10. Buy some new clothes. Whenever I hit a sales slump I went and bought a new suit. It made me feel like a million dollars and this seemed to get my sales going again.

Remember that all sales people have the occasional slump. If your confidence is at a low level, don't keep beating yourself up. Take some time to refocus, get back to the basics, have a holiday, have some fun, do a course or talk to some positive friends. Before you know it you will be well and truly back on track.

Action plan — What can I do right now to become the very best sales person that I can be?

IT'S A MARATHON, NOT A SPRINT

'Twenty years from now you will be more disappointed by the things you didn't do than by the things you did do. So throw off the bowlines! Sail away from the safe harbor. Catch the trade winds in your sails. Explore. Dream. Discover.'

Mark Twain

11 | Creating advertisements that sell

Advertising is an integral part of the selling process. Advertising is what we use to drive customers into our businesses. It is used to entice and motivate people to make contact with us and hopefully buy our products. It is incredibly complex, it is changing rapidly and even the largest advertising firms in the world are struggling with the changing advertising landscape.

Every day consumers are bombarded with tens of thousands of advertising messages from the internet, television, radio, newspapers, magazines and signs. For the businesses doing the advertising it is getting harder to be seen among the clutter. If your advertising doesn't get seen or heard, or your message isn't compelling enough to get the customer to act, you are simply throwing your money away.

It is impossible to cover in one section everything you need to know to make your advertising work, but I do cover some of the key things you need to do to drive more customers to your business. Then it's up to you to convert their interest into sales. (Another of my books, *101 Ways to Advertise Your Business*, is devoted entirely to advertising your business.)

82 If it doesn't get read, seen or heard it's a waste of time
83 Big outdoor signs create big impacts

101 WAYS TO SELL MORE OF ANYTHING TO ANYONE

84 Make people laugh
85 Use the power of testimonials to supercharge your advertising
86 Preach to the converted

#82 If it doesn't get read, seen or heard it's a waste of time

Today advertising has to cut through an enormous amount of clutter. It has to reach out, grab the customer's attention, shake them around and then get them to act. Too many advertisements get lost in the melee and this means they are a waste of time and money.

I see small business owners in particular spending a lot of time deciding if they should advertise in a particular area, and then spending very little time deciding what their advertisement should say. In my opinion it should be the other way around. We should all spend as much time as possible ensuring our advertisements are going to stand out, that the main messages are clear and easy to understand and that as many people as possible will read them.

Most advertising goes wrong in one or more of the following ways:

1. The advertisement (regardless of whether it is print or electronic) is too busy—there is too much in it, too many messages being sent.
2. The advertising is not attention grabbing—it is boring, plain or simply lacklustre.
3. It's not clear what needs to be done next or, in advertising jargon, there is no call to action.
4. It is all about the business, not what the business can do for the customer.
5. It is simply not compelling enough to make the customer respond. They may have read it or seen it but not acted on it.

My advice is simple. Regardless of what you are advertising or where you are advertising, if you follow this basic formula you will get far better results than if you don't. Here goes:

101 WAYS TO SELL MORE OF ANYTHING TO ANYONE

1. Create a big, bold heading or statement to catch your potential customers' attention—and I mean really big and bold.
2. Don't be afraid of white space or silence. In a cluttered world it is refreshing.
3. Outline why the customer should buy what you are selling.
4. Tell them what they need to do to buy it.
5. Close with a strong statement about why they should buy it.

This formula can be applied to radio, television, newspapers, the internet, signage—the lot. Follow these steps and you will get much greater value out of your advertising dollar because you will get more customers in the door.

#83 Big outdoor signs create big impacts

I am a big believer in the value of outdoor advertising in the form of signs. This example of the value of outdoor signage always makes me smile. An old lady who had owned the general store in a small town in Queensland for many years complained to me that all the tour buses drove straight past her store, as did the caravans and fishing convoys. She asked me for advice—the obvious solution was to give these people a compelling reason to stop.

Now this store was old so I asked the owner if it could possibly be the oldest general store in Queensland, and we agreed that it could be. (Okay, I am a marketing man and I never dig too deep for information just in case it's wrong.) An idea was starting to form in my head. I noticed that half the store was dark and dingy and wasn't used for day-to-day selling because it was full of old farming equipment and mining supplies or, in other words, it contained a treasure trove of memorabilia from a bygone era. In that decrepit part of the store were all the components of a delightful rustic museum.

So, as the plan unfolded, we organised for a sign to go outside the general store, stating it was the 'Oldest General Store in Queensland' and containing a line that said 'Museum—FREE Entry'. All of a sudden everyone was stopping there, getting their photos taken outside the 'Oldest General Store in Queensland' and, of course, while they were there they all grabbed an ice cream or a drink. This proved to be a very successful initiative and clearly not an overly complicated one.

Signs are powerful mediums. Billboards are enormously influential. The key is to create a compelling message, keep it really simple and easy to read, and give the customer a reason to buy.

#84 Make people laugh

If your advertising makes people laugh they are more likely to remember it. I love to laugh and I love to laugh a lot. I think most of us do. I believe that advertising that makes us laugh really strikes a chord in many people, hence the success of funny, quirky and even strange advertisements and television commercials (there are even television shows about them, which says it all).

If you can create advertising that puts a smile on people's faces you will be noticed. How you do that varies with each business type, but I suggest that you keep away from crude sexual innuendo (it's not really that funny anyway) and anything that could offend or alienate a large proportion of your target market. However, alienating some people can prove quite effective if it creates interest and discussion (i.e. word-of-mouth marketing). The following example illustrates this.

An unusual client of mine, a law firm, really embraces the idea of standing out from the crowd, of being different. They are not afraid of being unconventional and they certainly enjoy a laugh. Together we created a cheeky advertising campaign. We purchased a fantastic image of a pig, well a pig's bottom actually. Next to it we put the words 'So you don't think you need good legal advice?' Geddit? Subtle to some, subtle as a sledgehammer to others.

This little campaign of ours started with an advertisement in the local newspaper and now it is on billboards all over the place. Yep, there have been a few complaints from people feeling we are being disrespectful to pigs (which I just loved) and suggesting the advertisements didn't really promote the legal fraternity in a dignified way. Luckily my clients didn't back down from the pressure applied by the pig lovers or those concerned about lawyers' public standing, and now these advertisements have received international recognition. They have won awards, have ended up on the desk of every other

CREATING ADVERTISEMENTS THAT SELL

legal firm in Australia and have had a huge impact. The firm has grown from ten to thirty-five people in a couple of years. Did it work? Absolutely.

Get a laugh, be different and, most importantly, be bold when it comes to making your advertising stand out. The pig's bottom might be a little too much for you but there are many kinds of humour and it will generally break down barriers quicker than anything else.

#85 Use the power of testimonials to supercharge your advertising

Testimonials will add a whole new dimension to your advertising. The world's biggest companies use them all the time. Of course they can afford movie stars, sporting heroes, mountain climbers and retired politicians, people with high levels of credibility and appeal. Now while George Clooney may be a bit out of your budget, Mr Joe Average is not. Words of endorsement from a satisfied customer will carry a lot of weight in any advertising, because third party credibility is more powerful than anything a company can say about its own products or services.

The best way to elicit testimonials from your happy customers is to ask them. Tell them you would like their testimonial as long as they are comfortable giving it. I suggest that the business owner asks the customer and makes a big deal out of it. This shows that you respect them. Collect as many endorsements as you can and strike while the iron is hot. If someone contacts you regarding a great experience ask them then and there for a written testimonial.

Keep it short and punchy. Nobody wants to read a novel. If you want some ideas look at movie advertisements in newspapers. You will see that the testimonials used here are always short and sharp—it is the source of the quotes used that creates the impact. An example might be 'This is the movie of the decade', John Doe, *New York Times*. The power of this testimonial comes from the fact that the journalist who wrote the review is employed by the *New York Times*, a highly credible publication.

So, where possible, keep testimonials short, sweet and powerful. Include the name of the person who wrote the testimonial and, if appropriate, quote where they are from. Always get a person's approval before using testimonials, out of courtesy and because some organisations, particularly government departments, generally don't like their people endorsing products or services.

I recommend you use testimonials wherever you can—on your website, in your brochures, on your signage and in any other advertising you do.

#86 Preach to the converted

Existing customers are without doubt the best source of business for most of us. If they like what we do, they will happily try new products and services, they will recommend us to their families, friends and colleagues, and they remain our customers for as long as we keep meeting (and hopefully exceeding) their expectations.

Often, though, our existing customers are overlooked in the hunt for new customers. In fact, many businesses seem to push these loyal brethren out of the way, complaining all the time about how hard it is to find new customers.

My advice is to advertise and market to your existing customers as much as you can. Give them an incentive to continue using you by letting them know about special offers and sales before they are advertised to the broader community. Start a VIP club for your existing customers that lets them know about new products and services. Have special sales nights to which loyal customers are invited to get the best bargains up front. Send out a regular newsletter keeping your customers informed about what is going on in your business.

I believe that you are far better off selling more to your existing customers than spending a lot of money trying to reach new customers in complicated, confusing and unpredictable markets. Take the time to brainstorm ideas and ways to reach your existing customers more often and then implement a strategy to do this. I guarantee it will bring big results if done well. Treat your existing customers as special, which of course they are, and they will be advertising ambassadors for your business for many years to come.

Action plan — What can I do right now to become the very best sales person that I can be?

....
....
....
....
....
....
....
....
....
....
....
....
....
....
....
....
....
....
....
....
....
....
....
....
....

'The man who says it cannot be done should not interrupt the man doing it.'

Chinese proverb

12 | Learning a new language

Most of us have heard about body language. You may have read that over 80 per cent of communication (some people say over 90 per cent) is non-verbal. Meaning that it isn't what you say but how you say it and what you do that counts.

People described as 'sales naturals' don't actually have the gift of the gab as many think. In fact quite the opposite is true. They are normally exceptional observers who can read their customers very well. One of their greatest skills is being able to know what a person is thinking simply by watching them.

Body language is a broad topic. It is quite extraordinary in many ways and if you take the time to learn about it you will find that your overall levels of communication go through the roof. People will start to comment on what a great communicator you are, you will sell more, you will be liked more. The following tips will get you started but I strongly suggest that you read more widely about the concept. There are some excellent books devoted to understanding body language and Allan Pease is considered the world's leader. Alternatively, a quick Google search will point you in the direction of many valuable resources.

\# 87 Learn to tell when your customer is distracted
\# 88 Look for signs that they either like or dislike what they are hearing

101 WAYS TO SELL MORE OF ANYTHING TO ANYONE

\# 89 Mirroring, a simple technique that will improve your sales skills
\# 90 Don't set off the 'bullshit detector'

#87 Learn to tell when your customer is distracted

There is no point trying to sell anything to anyone if you haven't got their full attention. The key here is to be smart enough to know when the person you are talking to is distracted. Sometimes it's obvious, sometimes it isn't.

So how do you know when you have your customer's full attention? The best indicator is strong eye contact. When they are looking you in the eye, it is likely that they are listening to what you have to say. As soon as they start looking around, fidgeting or, even worse, checking their watch, you know you have lost their attention and need to get it back quickly.

One area where I notice sales people floundering is when they are talking to mothers or fathers with small children. Most children tend to go a little crazy when out shopping and as a result any parent has a limited capacity to listen to you because they have to keep one eye and one ear on the children. It is really hard to sell anything to anyone in this situation. Ask the parent if they would prefer that you contact them later. Even better, have a safe area where the kids can play so you can have an uninterrupted conversation.

When I was in the travel industry I made sales calls on various travel companies around the world. If I arrived at an office and the person I was meeting with seemed distracted I would stop and ask them if there was something wrong. I would say something like: 'You look a little distracted. Have I got you at a bad time or is what I am selling not of interest to you?' Generally this would snap them out of their preoccupation and nine times out of ten I would get an honest response that I could really work with. If they had something pressing on their mind that was unrelated to me and my products, I would suggest that we stop the meeting and that I come back later in the day, no matter how late, to talk to them. In the meantime they could attend to whatever was distracting them.

Most of the time this suggestion was met with relief and gratitude. Often it was the basis for developing some really positive relationships. They knew I had travelled many kilometres to see them, yet I would let them get on with what they had to do and we could then have a committed and connected meeting at a time to suit them, without distraction. How do you think these people responded to what I was selling? Very positively and I got most of my best clients from relationships that started like this.

Sadly many sales people do the complete opposite. They detect that the customer is distracted but they plough on regardless. In fact they may even speed up the presentation, leaving out vital information, because they feel the customer wants them gone. Sometimes this may be true, but you need to know why they want you out. Is it that they have a completely unrelated matter they need to attend to? Or is it that they have a problem with whatever it is you are trying to sell them? If it is the latter, and you can persuade the customer to tell you what the problem is, you can at least address their concerns and, if you are convincing and genuine, take this opportunity to turn them around.

Learn to tell when your customer is distracted and do whatever you can to get their attention. Read their signals, don't be afraid to ask them questions and give them solutions that will help them. Do this and you will be well on the way to building strong relationships with your customers that will pay off for many years to come.

#88 Look for signs that they either like or dislike what they are hearing

When we are talking to a person, or selling to them, it is very handy if we can tell that they like what we are saying or, more importantly, that they don't like what we are saying. So how can body language tell us this? There are a few sure-fire signals for both and a good sales person will learn to react quickly to both positive and negative signals.

Here are some signs that the customer likes or agrees with what you are saying:

1. They nod their head a lot.
2. They maintain strong and direct eye contact.
3. They are focused on your presentation and not distracted by things going on around them.
4. They sit still and in an upright position.
5. They smile.
6. They look contemplative, even placing a hand on the chin.
7. They have an open body (arms not crossed).
8. They lean in towards you.

Body language signs that the customer doesn't agree with you or doesn't like what you are saying include the following:

1. They shake their heads when they should be nodding.
2. They don't often make eye contact and they look around the room a lot.
3. They rub the back of their neck (what you are saying is giving them a pain in the neck).
4. They may either slouch in the chair or look like they are about to leap out of the chair and run away.
5. They smile insincerely.

6. They cross their arms and lean back.
7. They look at their watch (a lot).

A good sales person reads the signs and responds accordingly. If you are getting plenty of positive body language messages you know you are doing the right thing. If you are not, then quickly change what you are doing because you are about to lose the customer. It is a waste of time trying to sell to someone whose body language shows that they have completely shut off.

#89 Mirroring, a simple technique that will improve your sales skills

Body mirroring is a fantastic body language skill. So what does it involve?

Think about spending time with someone you really like. You are both engrossed in the conversation. As you sit across from each other, something strange will happen. You will start to copy each other's body movements. For example, you will move so you are sitting in the same position. If you put your hands behind your head and lean back, wait a few moments and the person you are talking to will put their hands behind their head. We do it subconsciously, but we all do it. Next time you are enjoying a coffee in a crowded cafe, look for two people who are engrossed in conversation. If they start to mirror each other's movements and mannerisms, you will know that they both like each other and what is being said.

How can this phenomenon help us in a sales environment? Well, if you are presenting and the customer starts to mirror your movements, this tells you that they like you and what you are selling. This is called a positive selling signal. If they sit across from you with their arms crossed, looking as though they may leap out of their chair at any moment and beat you to death with a stapler, there is a good chance that you are not resonating or connecting with them at quite the level you would like to.

If you want someone to like you a little quicker, you can consciously mirror his or her movements. Some people may find this a little manipulative. For me it is the same as being prepared and doing a good sales presentation. It is a technique in your sales toolbox that can be used to put people at ease and to build their confidence in you.

Using body language effectively takes time. I suggest that before you start running around copying everyone's movements and doing mirror impersonations that you spend some time just observing people and reading some body language books. There is no doubt that body language provides insights into what a person is feeling and thinking. The more you learn about it, the better equipped you will be to read your customers.

#90 Don't set off the 'bullshit detector'

I rarely use swear words in my books—I save them up for real-life situations. But I can think of no better term than 'bullshit detector' for that mechanism which goes off in our brains when we hear something that doesn't sound quite true. We all have them though some of us have more finely tuned ones than others.

Sales people are often stereotyped as fast talking, smooth and not overly truthful. Sure, a few are and many more used to be. But this kind of sales person really doesn't succeed today—consumers have become too smart and this type of sales approach is more likely to drive them away.

Try this as an exercise. When you are out and about buying things, get in touch with your own bullshit detector. Note how you feel if a sales person is less than honest, or too smooth, or too pushy. This is how your customer will feel if you sell in this way.

So how do our bullshit detectors work? We take in a huge amount of information when we stand face to face with another human being. Slight movements, language tone and volume, eye contact and lots of other subtle signals all get used by our brain to make a decision about what we are being told.

What is the possibility of being a long-term, highly successful sales professional if you trigger your potential customers' bullshit detector? Not flaming much!

If you are reading this and wondering if you do set off the odd alarm in your customers, then you are probably guilty of bullshitting and the best thing to do is stop it immediately. Perhaps you are one of those unfortunate folk who appear to be bullshitting even when you are not. How do you find out what people think of you? Ask them. Ask your friends, colleagues, family and even your customers. Ask them how they feel about the way you sell, whether you sound honest and open, what your greatest strengths and greatest weaknesses are.

This is a very enlightening exercise. You have to ask people whom you trust and respect and you have to ask them to be honest. But most importantly, you have to be prepared to listen to what they have to say—the good and the bad.

If you are brave enough to ask people these questions you will learn more about yourself in one conversation than you have probably learnt in the last year. I do this exercise every few years. It certainly makes me a better sales person, and a better human being.

Action plan — What can I do right now to become the very best sales person I can be?

'It is not the mountain that we conquer, but ourselves.'
Sir Edmund Hillary

13 | Developing your own style

There is a lot of information in this book that will certainly help anyone become a better sales person. And of course you can find a wealth of material on selling in other books, on websites, in training seminars, and so on. In fact it is easy to get a little overwhelmed by all this information. What we need to do is to use it to develop our own style. Adopt the right skills and techniques but use the ones that suit you. That is what will truly make you a success in this field and, importantly, will make you feel true to yourself. When I first started reading about selling I found myself trying to imitate the people I was reading about. But it never seemed to sit right with me and sometimes I actually felt like a fraud. Then I realised that it was important to adapt the experts' recommendations, advice and technical expertise to suit my own personal style. That is when my sales career really kicked off. This section includes ways to further improve your skills and advice on how to build your own style to get the results you want.

91 Work on your reputation
92 Become a resource for your clients
93 Always respect your clients
94 Be yourself
95 You can never read enough sales books
96 Do regular sales training

101 WAYS TO SELL MORE OF ANYTHING TO ANYONE

\# 97 Grow with your customers
\# 98 Do what others won't do
\# 99 Use what you sell
\#100 Be detached from the outcome—customers smell desperation
\#101 Have an extraordinary amount of fun

#91 Work on your reputation

As a sales professional you take two significant things with you every time you change jobs or start a new business: experience and your reputation. A great reputation can take years to build but can be destroyed in minutes. Therefore, it should be treasured and protected at all times.

I aim to have a reputation for being honest, ethical, professional, respectful and, ideally, fun to deal with. What sort of reputation do you want to have? If you are not sure, try the following exercise. I started doing it when I was in my early twenties and I continue to do it on a regular basis. Think about the people that you respect. They may or may not be people you know personally. Ask yourself what it is about these people that you admire and respect, and then write these qualities down. Which of these qualities do you have or wish you had? This list of qualities will provide you with a guide as to the reputation you want to have. Your actions, both personal and professional, will help you build it.

#92 Become a resource for your clients

I have a very good friend who is a very successful sales representative for a television station. He earns great money and he gets the best clients. He has built a wonderful relationship with his clients by becoming a central resource for them. While his job is to sell advertising space on the television station, he goes above and beyond that by offering advice to his clients on any aspect of marketing. He shares his views and opinions both openly and honestly and because of this his clients know they can trust him. The end result is that he has become a valuable asset to most of his clients and the pay-off is that they book all of their television advertising through him.

This is a great way to increase your sales, but it takes time and you have to be genuinely interested in your customers. My friend will meet his clients for coffee, spend an hour or two talking to them about their issues, and leave without ever mentioning his television station.

Help your customers in any way possible and they will love you, respect you and buy from you. Look for ways to help them build their business. Recently I was contacted by the general manager of a company that prints calendars. The company has thousands of customers around Australia and New Zealand and hundreds of sales reps. He wanted to give his customers a gift that would help them to grow their business and at the same time give his sales reps credibility. He ordered 10,000 copies of one of my books, *101 Ways to Advertise Your Business*, and the sales reps gave copies out to all of their customers.

Look for ways to help your customers however you can, and you will build very long and solid relationships with them.

#93 Always respect your clients

Even if you are older, wiser and more experienced than your customers, always show them respect. Respect is essential for success in the world of sales. I have learnt this from working with older sales people, most of whom started selling in times that were much less complicated. The one characteristic that they all share is that they show total respect for their customers. They show it in a number of ways:

1. They use the customer's title and surname (Mr Griffiths, Miss Andrews) even if they are older than the customer.
2. They are considerate—they offer a seat to their customers, or perhaps a glass of water or anything else that will make the customer feel more respected.
3. They don't waste the customer's time.

Some people struggle with the concept of respect—they feel that it is demeaning in some way to call a person 'Sir' or 'Madam'. I feel that we should always show this level of respect and while this might make me seem somewhat old-fashioned, this approach has worked on many levels for me. That said, showing respect to my customers is a sincere act—I do respect them. I value them and I want to build a relationship with them.

Respect is a powerful thing. If you sincerely respect your customers you will become one of a very small group of elite and successful sales people.

#94 Be yourself

It is easy to lose ourselves a little when we are in a sales role. Sometimes we change to become like the people around us, sometimes we change to reflect the product we are selling and sometimes we take on the identity of the business. This is all okay, but regardless of what you are selling I believe that it is really important to be yourself.

There is nothing to be gained by becoming a clone. By all means learn from those around you, embrace the vision of the company you are working for, or set the vision of your own business, but always keep your own personality, your own values and your own style close by. There is an old saying in the world of sales that people buy the person first and the product second and while this may not always be true, it is certainly true a lot of the time.

The exception to the rule of being yourself is that if you have certain personality traits that don't aid your sales career then these will need to change. For example, if you have a 'well that's me, take it or leave it' attitude that leads you to dress like a slob, you probably will be left! I have strongly promoted throughout this book the concept of constant and never-ending improvement and that to me is the key to not only being a better sales person but being a better human being.

Be yourself in the world of sales. Don't try to be someone you're not—your customers will see through you in a heartbeat. I believe that I really found my stride in the world of sales when I stopped trying to be someone else and I let my own personality shine through.

#95 You can never read enough sales books

There are some incredible sales books on the market, thousands of them. Some cover the entire sales field, while others cover specific aspects like 'closing the sale' or 'generating sales leads'. There are industry-specific sales books, online selling books, books on face-to-face selling and so on.

My advice is to build your own library of sales-related titles. (I have included a list of the ones that I have found most helpful in the back of this book.) Buy different types, different styles, from simple books to more complex ones, and by different authors. Read them often. Glance through them or read them cover to cover, and when you come across something that strikes a chord, bookmark it. I actually keep a computer reference file that helps me find particular information or pages in specific books so I don't have to keep rummaging through 100 or so titles every time I want to find a certain article.

I am a very big fan of Dale Carnegie, in particular his book *How to Win Friends and Influence People*. I have read it at least fifty times. Why? Because every single time I read it I pick up something new that for some reason didn't seem so significant in the past. I realise that things change and what is important to me now may not have been important in the past. People say the same thing about all of the books in my *101 Ways* series. Every time they read one they pick up something new. That is a great compliment to me. If you read a book once, get all of the information out of it and then throw it away I somehow feel that it is lacking.

Another fabulous tool is the audio book. I love them. My iPod is jam-packed with audio books and I always have a few CDs in the car for those trips of an hour or more. They are a great way to learn while doing other things and I really like hearing the author's voice. You can pick up so many extra bits and pieces from an audio book that you just don't get out of a hard-copy book (and I guess vice versa).

#96 Do regular sales training

Regardless of how long you have been selling, you can always learn something new. If you think you can't, you're in big trouble. In the last ten years there has been a big increase in the number of specialist training organisations running all kinds of courses, from full-year programs to one-day seminars. There are also businesses that offer sales coaching to individuals on a one-on-one basis. Clearly you need to determine what you would specifically like to learn about or which sales areas you need to work on and then find a training program to suit. Regardless of the type of training program you choose to attend, do it on a regular basis, at least once a year.

When starting a training program, I strongly suggest you leave your ego at the door and enter with an open mind. I have run a lot of sales training programs over the years and there is a certain kind of participant who drives me crazy. They have generally been in a sales role for some time and they seem to think they have all of the answers. They come to the seminar with a completely closed mind and with no real desire to learn, but with a need to show others how much they know. We've all seen this kind of person and they are frustrating for everyone. I feel for them because if they simply lightened up and accepted that they could learn something they could become so much better at what they do.

So spend the time and the money to do ongoing sales training on a regular basis. Enter every program with an open mind and be an active participant; share what you have learnt and be prepared to learn from others. If you want specific help, I strongly suggest sourcing a sales coach. They can help you to resolve specific issues or tailor a program to help you achieve your goals.

#97 Grow with your customers

A great sales person develops a long-term relationship with their clients. If that client is a business, it is likely that the business will grow. I have seen many sales people lose their best customers simply because they didn't grow at the same pace. The customer needed different products, more volume, more after-sale service or greater flexibility in the buying process, and the sales business couldn't keep up. As a result they lost the account.

To grow we need to see ourselves and our customers as part of a team. We need to know where our clients are heading, what their long-term needs and expectations are. We have to put our own plans into place to make sure we can meet these, and we must grow at the same pace as our clients.

Remember too that as our customers grow, our competitors will be trying to get the business from us. If the customer starts to lose confidence in your firm's ability to support them and grow with them they may start to look elsewhere.

Try to develop the type of relationship with your customers which allows you to work together and openly and honestly discuss their growth plans. You may be surprised by how open people are to this concept and by how appreciative they will be of your proactive stance.

#98 Do what others won't do

I have always tried to live by this philosophy and I have encountered many successful people who do the same. There is a real power to be had by standing out from the crowd, being different and going the extra mile. How you are different is up to you, but actions speak louder than words.

I remember reading about an amazing car salesman who used to send cards to his customers at a time when this was an unusual thing to do. He sent birthday cards, anniversary cards, Christmas cards, Easter cards and so on. Over a period of some thirty years in the industry he built up quite a list of customers. In fact he was sending out thousands of cards every year. He made a point of always writing them himself and he always personalised each message. Now this salesman sold more cars than any other sales person ever. He received a huge number of word-of-mouth referrals and there were many families to whom he sold new cars to three generations. Standing out is important, but being prepared to go the extra mile is even more important.

Do a review of the people in your industry who sell the same things that you do. Generally most sales people within an industry start to look the same and act the same. The things they believe they can do and the things they believe they can't do are the same. They have the same blinkers on.

Look for ways to do things that your competitors can't or won't do. This will make you memorable and will win you customers, plenty of them.

It isn't often that we are really impressed by sales people. In fact we generally expect to be underwhelmed and I usually am. What a wonderful opportunity every single sales person has to be different. An example that really surprised me recently came from a very unexpected quarter. I have always used a particular credit card to pay all my business and travel expenses. It's easy, generally accepted all over the world and the statements make it easy for my accounts people to allocate costs in the appropriate places. Then one month, due to some mix-up, I was late paying a big credit card bill and I was charged a penalty of $700. It really bugged me but I knew the rules and I copped it on the chin.

A few weeks later I received a call from a sales person at the credit card company. She wanted to sell me something related to the card, but I wasn't interested. She accepted that and ended the conversation by asking me if there was anything else she could help me with. I used the opportunity to express my disappointment at being charged a penalty after paying my bills on time for the last fifteen years. To my surprise, the woman agreed. She put me on hold for a few minutes, then came back and told me that they would waive the charge and that they were very sorry for putting it on in the first place. I was stunned.

Look for ways to do what others don't and you will become a sales legend!

#99 Use what you sell

For me there is nothing quite as strange as having someone trying to sell me something that they don't use themselves. In the world of network marketing, this is a key principle: use the products you are trying to sell. There are two reasons to do this.

First, you get to know the products thoroughly. Reading a brochure will only get you so far. Actually using a product every day will really highlight both the strengths and the weaknesses, which will make it much easier to honestly sell any product.

The second reason to use what you sell is so that you can tell your customers that you do. There is no better testimonial than that the person who sells the product also uses the product. If you don't use it, what do you do if the customer asks you if you use it?

Of course if you don't use the product for some specific reason you may need to ask yourself why you are trying to sell it. Believing in what we sell is vitally important to be successful when selling it.

#100 Be detached from the outcome — customers smell desperation

I've had sales people come into my office and literally beg me for a sale, saying if they didn't get this sale they would lose their job.

This is an extreme example, but I will let you in on a secret. No matter how good you think you are at hiding desperation, our human sixth sense can smell it a mile away — and most of us run from it. Regardless of just how desperate you actually may be, it is imperative to clear your head and be detached from the outcome of any sales interaction. Let me explain.

Through a strange set of circumstances I found myself selling encyclopaedias door-to-door around Australia when I was in my early twenties. My first port of call was Tasmania, in the middle of winter. As the last stop before Antarctica, it is very cold. My job was to go around specific neighbourhoods at around 5 p.m., knocking on doors and trying to sell sets of encyclopaedias. I had no money at all, and this job was totally commission based. The first few weeks were really tough. I was desperate, I needed to make money to eat, I was freezing and I had a host of other crazy things going on in my life. I was desperate and I am sure it showed. The result — zero sales.

I soon realised that I needed to change my attitude. I was too needy and desperate and the one thing that the people of Tasmania were not going to do is let some strange, forlorn-looking man with desperation in his eyes into their homes, after dark and in the middle of winter.

So I spent half an hour each day getting mentally prepared before hitting the road. I visualised a full belly, my troubles all gone and introducing myself to some of the nice folks in the area and giving them the opportunity to help their kids get the very best education they could. I changed from being a deranged desperado to a bright, positive and cheery young man, offering help to young families. As you can imagine I started to sell my encyclopaedias and lots of them.

The key here is to really believe in what you are thinking. I did realise that yes, I was broke, but I was getting by somehow. Yes, I had problems to deal with but they could be a heck of a lot worse. And yes, I did believe that the books I was selling really would help these people. The results spoke for themselves.

#101 Have an extraordinary amount of fun

This seems the perfect note to finish on (well, before you get to the twenty bonus tips at least). I think many of us take business and life far too seriously, particularly business. Why shouldn't we have fun doing what we do? In fact I think it should be mandatory. Business is simply not that important. Now I know that statement is heresy to some of you and, as a reforming workaholic, I know just how important we think our businesses are. But in reality it is just another part of our lives and yes, it helps put the food on the table but surely it needs to be so much more. It should be a way to learn, to grow, to develop deep and connected relationships with other people, to make a difference to the planet and those around us and to give us joy. When did it become so serious?

This may sound kind of clichéd, but people who absolutely love what they do, regardless of what it is, have a glow and a radiance about them that rubs off on those they come into contact with. They are quick to smile and quick to laugh and this is infectious. Who can have a lousy day when you have lots of fun all the time?

For those of you running your own business or in a selling role, if it doesn't bring you joy, then get out and find something that does. My very best piece of advice is to have as much fun selling as you possibly can. Don't get stressed about selling. Lighten up, laugh a lot, make other people laugh. Enjoy what you do and look for ways to have more fun every single day of your life.

Action plan—What can I do right now to become the very best sales person that I can be?

DEVELOPING YOUR OWN STYLE

'The price of excellence is discipline. The cost of mediocrity is disappointment.'

William Ward

20 bonus tips to help you sell more of anything

In every book in the *101 Ways* series I always make a point of including some bonus tips, the icing on the cake. Hopefully by now you have picked up lots of great ideas to help you sell more of anything. Enjoy these tips. None are more or less important than each other but they will all help you become the sales person that you want to be.

#102 Send articles from newspapers
#103 Reward people for giving you a lead
#104 Sometimes it pays to 'down sell'
#105 Develop a genuine interest in people — you may be surprised
#106 Ask your customers for their ideas
#107 Visualise the outcome
#108 Be a high quality corporate citizen and tell your customers that you are
#109 Don't be afraid to talk about money
#110 Use food to sell more of anything
#111 Share your life with your customers
#112 Be accessible to your customers
#113 Have a moaning buddy
#114 Is your business customer friendly?
#115 Mystery shop another business
#116 Do a public speaking course

101 WAYS TO SELL MORE OF ANYTHING TO ANYONE

#117 Share company victories with your customers
#118 If you are confident enough, let your customers try your product
#119 Pick up the cost of the call
#120 Make it really easy for people to pay you
#121 Register a clever domain name

#102 Send articles from newspapers

To build long-term, valued relationships with our customers we need to go above and beyond the call of duty. I like to send my customers newspaper and magazine articles I come across that I know will be of interest to them. It only takes a few minutes and I find it incredibly effective.

There are two reasons why I do this. First and foremost because I really do have a strong desire to help people build successful businesses. As mentioned before, I think this sincerity is really important in anything to do with selling. Second, I feel that my customers like the attention and the fact that I clearly think of them outside our meetings or our time working together.

Putting some effort into building relationships with customers is rewarding on every level. I suggest that you develop your own unique way of going the extra mile with your customers.

#103 Reward people for giving you a lead

I think there is great value in spending money to thank someone for referring business to you. Personally I don't like the structured approach where you get a specific amount of cash for every referral but it is a matter of deciding what works for you. I like to send small gifts to people who recommend customers to me—perhaps a bottle of wine, tickets to the movies, a book, some chocolates or a gift voucher of some sort. It doesn't cost very much but it means a lot to the people who receive the gift and it is a way for me to say thank you.

Being a little creative can be a good idea. Spend some time looking for unusual thank-you gifts, go out of your way to give people something that they will really like and you are bound to make a strong impression. But, most importantly, be sincere not mechanical in your gratitude. Whenever possible, make a point of personally thanking people who refer you business. I think we should all make the time to do this more often.

#104 Sometimes it pays to 'down sell'

No doubt you are well and truly familiar with the term 'up selling' but what is 'down selling' and why on earth would you want to do it? Well, it is part of being a great sales person and only the great ones can really do it.

At some stage in your sales career you will encounter someone who wants to buy way too much of whatever you are selling or who wants to buy something which is wrong for them. You know it is too much or that it won't work, and you will have to make a split-second decision—do you tell them or do you let them make the purchase?

Of course the right thing to do is to tell them and give them your advice; in other words, to down sell. If they still want to make the purchase, at least you will have done the right thing, but if they realise that you are right and that you have saved them from making a big mistake, they'll be your fans for life.

Ethical sales people last a long time in their industry and they enjoy great success. Think about how you would handle this situation if you haven't encountered it yet. If you have already experienced it, what did you do? Never be afraid to down sell to a customer in order to build a long-term relationship.

#105 Develop a genuine interest in people—you may be surprised

Although Dale Carnegie was writing motivational books and inspiring tens of thousands of people in the 1930s, his ideas are even more relevant today. Dale Carnegie promoted the importance of being genuinely interested in people. Unfortunately most people's primary concern is themselves and they want the universe to revolve around them. This may sound harsh but I think it is true. By focusing outwards instead of inwards, our perception changes. If you take a very real and genuine interest in the people you encounter they will pick up on this and be extremely receptive. It is the way to build friendships and relationships. You have to leave your ego at the door and encourage people to open up and talk about themselves. It often takes time but when you do, you find out some amazing things.

I love people. I meet a lot of them and I believe that every single one has a great story to tell. I go into every sales meeting with a desire to learn about the person or the people I will be talking to. This is my primary thought. Sure, I want to sell to them and I hope they will decide to buy from me, but if they don't I'll be happy to have met some new people whom I am sure I can learn something from.

If you find that you are not that interested in the people you are selling to, try this experiment. Spend one day making the effort to talk to people, to connect with them. Try to get them to tell you something about themselves. I think you will find that your attitude to them will change as they open up.

Now I am not saying that we should do this to be manipulative—quite the opposite. Do it to be a genuine human being. Any other benefit that results is a magnificent bonus.

#106 Ask your customers for their ideas

Customers can be an amazing source of profitable information. The problem is that most people are afraid to ask their customers for their opinions. Often this is because they are afraid of what their customers might say.

I am no different. I recently had all of my past and present clients surveyed. Despite the excellent relationships I have with them, and the very open and honest communication, I felt a similar nervousness, imagining all the things they would complain about. Fortunately, the feedback proved I had no reason to be nervous.

Some of the best ideas for improving sales could be right under your nose, but you simply can't see them because you are too close to your business. Talk to some of your best customers. Go and see them or take them out for a coffee. Ask them to give you ideas and recommendations to improve your business in any way possible. You may be surprised by the responses and the ideas they give you.

I came across a hardware store that ran a competition each week. They offered a $50 gift voucher for the best idea on how to improve their business. It was open to both staff and customers and they got many great ideas that made them a lot of money. Clearly this was a very smart and simple way to get a host of people working to build their business.

Everyone looks at situations slightly differently. There could be a million-dollar idea in the head of one of your customers but they haven't told you about it because they don't think you would be interested.

#107 Visualise the outcome

As you may have gathered while reading the various tips in this book I am a big believer in setting goals and taking a positive and proactive approach to selling. I like to go one step further and visualise the outcome of every sales interaction that I have. I like to create a mental picture of the customer saying yes (if I haven't met them I use movie stars to create my mental picture).

When you go into a meeting with a positive attitude and a sense of wellbeing because you feel that the outcome is going to be positive, it generally ends up that way. If you go into a meeting feeling worried, panicky, stressed or freaked out about what will happen, you tend to leave the same way.

I believe in the power of visualisation and I encourage you to try it. It won't always work, but I find that the more effort I put into getting mentally prepared before a sales call the more often I get the result I want.

#108 Be a high quality corporate citizen and tell your customers that you are

I believe it is our duty to be great corporate citizens and then to be proud enough to tell everyone that we are. Our customers expect this of us, both as individuals and as an organisation.

So what is a high quality corporate citizen? To me it is an organisation or an individual who is generous with their time, their money and their expertise, or a combination of all three, and who gives these resources to help those in the community who are less fortunate.

We have a responsibility to the communities in which we make our living, a responsibility to give help to those who need it. I know there are government and not-for-profit organisations set up to help those in need but they can't do it all.

Writing a cheque is nice but giving up your time and rolling up your sleeves is even better. Get involved in your community however you feel best able to and don't be afraid to tell your customers, your staff, your family and friends and anyone else who will listen. It is something to be proud of and the more people you tell, the more people who may do likewise.

#109 Don't be afraid to talk about money

There are many people around who don't like to talk money. I am actually one of them, especially when I am selling my own services. I prefer to send through a quote to a customer after our meeting rather than talk about money in the middle of a meeting. I have worked hard to change this attitude as I see it as a hindrance to doing business.

You need to be able to talk about money. You need to be able to negotiate with clients if that is the type of business you sell for. Like anything, the more you do it the more at ease you tend to get. I work hard to bring costs into a conversation, talking about it in a matter-of-fact way. Generally for most clients seeking professional services like marketing, legal or accounting, the cost is at the top of the list of things they want to know, so why beat around the bush? Open up and start talking about it.

If you really are a 'money-phobe', work off a price list. That way you are simply relaying the information on the sheet in front of you. This can send a message that these prices are set and out of your hands; your job is to tell the customer about the product or service.

If you are very comfortable talking money, be careful in case your customers are not so comfortable. Be a little gentle, talk softer, read their feelings and learn to look for 'money-phobes' so you can put them at ease.

#110 Use food to sell more of anything

I have sold more things using food as a 'bribe' than any other sales technique. I have bought thousands of boxes of chocolates, tens of thousands of cups of coffee, cakes by the truck load, containers of mangoes and everything else in between.

Food is a beautiful gift. It is engaging and it is something we can all relate to. I often take food to sales presentations for all to share or to leave as a gift. I make a point of buying enough for the entire office, which sometimes takes a little detective work, but it pays off.

Food breaks down many barriers. I have had some fun with very serious senior executive teams in big corporations by turning them into compliant puppies over a box of doughnuts. Sounds ridiculously simple and it is.

One thing I always try to do is never buy treats from food stores close to the business I am seeing. Other people may buy their food bribes from there and the people getting the bribes are more than likely sick of getting the same things over and over. I always buy from a bakery on the other side of town, and I buy their specialty, the thing that is unlikely to be available from other bakeries.

Be imaginative, reward people for seeing you, buy good food and plenty of it and you will always be welcomed back and you will get the business you are chasing, sooner or later.

#111 Share your life with your customers

A lot of sales people are quite bland. I mean this in the nicest possible way. They are professional, they are polite, but they resemble sales robots. Just as I am interested in my customers, I like to know a bit about the people who are selling to me. I want to know something about their interests and what their passions in life are. It makes the sales person appear much more human and it helps to build a connection.

I had a printing rep call on me not so long ago. She had a great portfolio of print samples, different-sized brochures and posters and a host of other assorted material. Each of the items had pictures of African animals printed on them and the photographs were quite extraordinary. As a photography lover I asked her about the images and she proudly told me that they were all hers. She was a mad keen amateur photographer and these images were taken on a series of holidays. Her eyes lit up, her smile was beaming and she shared with me not only her love of photography but also of wildlife. I felt a beautiful connection with this lady and she became much more effective as a sales representative when she shared her passion.

I think all sales people can share something of themselves. If you have a hobby, be proud of it. If you play sports, wear a badge promoting it. Show that you are human. If you have kids, keep a photo handy and don't hesitate to show it to your customers. Let them into your life and let them see that you are just like them and that you have dreams and aspirations and a life outside of what you are doing.

Some sales people tend to feel that this is being unprofessional. I feel that it is being real, open and sincere, and that beats professionalism hands down every time in my book.

#112 Be accessible to your customers

If you want to keep your customers buying from you it is important that they can reach you easily. All too often I see sales people who start climbing the corporate ladder only to lose touch with their customers. They become too difficult to communicate with and ultimately their customers find someone else to buy from.

Accessibility doesn't mean that you have to be on call twenty-four hours a day. It does mean that your customers have to know that you are still looking after them even if you don't actually deal with them on a daily basis. Many customers feel a real sense of connection with their sales people and they can feel betrayed when the sales people are no longer there for them. Once again, it is all a matter of communication, the eternal and constant driving force in the world of sales.

Small business owners in particular seem to struggle with this concept as their business grows. When they start the business they can't seem to do enough for their customers. But then they spend more and more time in the 'back office' doing paperwork, running the business, managing the staff, buying the stock and doing everything but interacting with their customers. Clearly this is a bit confusing for the customers and it is a good way to lose business.

You can determine how accessible you are going to be to your customers by setting boundaries, but beware of the trap of looking inwards at your business and not outwards at your customers. Be as accessible as possible. Communicate with your customers and let them know that you are always going to be there if they need you. Most importantly of all, only send this message if you really mean it.

#113 Have a moaning buddy

Several years ago I was presenting at a conference called 'The Road to Success'. It was a very inspirational event, with lots of people coming from all over Australia to work on ways of becoming as successful as they possibly could. The MC was a fantastic speaker called Murray Jorgensen, a true statesman with a light style and a strong message. At the beginning of the conference he made the following statement:

> At conferences things sometimes go wrong. The coffee can be cold, the speakers late, the fish undercooked, the toilets grubby and so on. It is easy to lose sight of why we are all here and to start complaining to anyone who will listen about all of the things that are wrong. But rather than do that, I want you to find someone in the room and they are going to be your moaning buddy. Every time you see them, get all of your moaning over and done with so you can actually focus on learning and growing. With everyone else you encounter, be positive, energetic and enthusiastic.

So we all found a moaning buddy and had a good whinge about life, work, the excessively cold room, the war in Iraq and so on. Then we went about our day. Whenever we encountered our moaning buddy we had a good moan and a great belly laugh.

This was a very interesting exercise. For starters it really did get the negativity out of the way. It demonstrated that we can be positive and enthusiastic most of the time if we want to be, that attitude is a state of mind.

I think the same should apply in everyday life. We should all have moaning buddies we can contact when we need to vent—get it over and done with, have a great laugh and then get on with the business of living and enjoying every moment of every day.

I hope you find your moaning buddy.

#114 Is your business customer friendly?

Now this may sound like a strange tip to have in a sales book, but if your business isn't customer friendly, how on earth can you sell anything? A surprising number of businesses don't really get this point. They spend a fortune on advertising, trying to get new customers, yet they don't look after their existing ones, they don't answer the phone, they don't deliver on their promises and so on.

So what does it mean to be customer friendly? Here are my views on what makes a customer-friendly business:

1. Customers are considered the number-one priority by all members of staff. They are treated with absolute respect, everything possible is done to accommodate them, to serve them and to exceed their expectations in every way.
2. A customer-friendly business has policies that encourage customers to do business with them. It isn't laden with policies about what the business won't do.
3. The business is clean, tidy, easy to find, and open at hours that are convenient to the customer.
4. The business has a 'yes' attitude rather than an automatic 'no' attitude.
5. There are lots of little things that say 'we care'—a place for the kids to play, drinking water, a place to sit, great magazines, convenient change rooms or a host of other things depending on the type of business.
6. Calls are returned.
7. Follow-up is done, and done on time.
8. The business under promises and over delivers—consistently.
9. The staff are happy, friendly and polite—and you can tell that they like working there.
10. The business is constantly getting better at what it does.

There are business owners who think all of these things are just a waste of time and money—seriously. I don't understand why but I say fantastic, because the more of them there are, the easier it is for us to stand out from the crowd. Do whatever you can to be the ultimate customer-friendly business and your customers will reward you every day.

#115 Mystery shop another business

You may have heard about mystery shopping as a tool for identifying where a business is going right and where it is going wrong. An external company sends a person to survey the business and report back to the business owner with the results. Mystery shopping is a great business development tool and while it is predominantly used in the retail environment I believe every business should use it.

So by all means get your own business mystery shopped but, as an interim exercise, I suggest you informally mystery shop someone else's business. There are lots of things that can be evaluated, and you can tailor your list to suit the business you choose, but here are some ideas:

1. How easy is it to find their telephone number?
2. How do they handle your telephone enquiry?
3. How easy is it to find the company website (assuming they have one)?
4. How easy is it to find the business?
5. Is it well lit?
6. Is it inviting?
7. Is it clean inside and out?
8. How are the staff presented?
9. Is it easy to find your way around?
10. Does anyone welcome you?
11. Does anyone ask if you need help?
12. What are their sales skills like?
13. Did they give you what you needed?
14. How was their pricing?
15. Did they thank you for making the purchase?
16. Did they do anything above and beyond the call of duty?
17. Would you use this business again?
18. Would you recommend it to your friends?

So why go through all of this? What's in it for you? The pay-off is that you will look at your own business in a whole new light once you do this exercise. It hones your observation skills and makes you aware of the many aspects of a business that contribute to the overall level of customer service.

Open your eyes, become a mystery shopper and see how your perspective changes in every way.

#116 Do a public speaking course

I did my first public speaking course when I was about fifteen and I am still doing them at the age of forty-three. My first public speaking course was a great confidence boost. I don't really remember why I did it, but I ended up on the school debating team, doing my best to out-perform competing teams and learning to think fast on my feet.

These skills served me well in my working life. I learnt to be organised and to be prepared before any meeting or presentation. I learnt to make strong and compelling arguments. I gained confidence and felt more comfortable talking in front of a group of strangers. And I learnt how to rebuff protests.

So, if you haven't already, sign up for a public speaking course. There are plenty of them around. Toastmasters is an international group that is very well known (www.toastmasters.org). It will be a great investment of time and energy and I don't think it is ever too late to learn. I intend to continue doing public speaking courses until I am too old to talk.

#117 Share company victories with your customers

Everyone loves a winner and people buy from winners. If your company wins an award, lands a big contract, expands, celebrates a birthday or makes a donation, tell your customers all about it.

You can do this on your website, in your brochures, with signs, face to face or just about any other way imaginable. If you are an award-winning business put it all over your stationery, your vehicles and your advertising. It does carry enormous clout and I also think it helps promote a healthy sense of pride in the business in all the staff.

You should include any of these victories in your sales presentations to add credibility to your business and your products or services. Use whatever you can to build a compelling case for customers to buy from you—these victories will certainly help.

If your business doesn't bother to enter awards it should. I know it takes time and energy and costs money to prepare a submission, but if you have two businesses selling similar products at similar prices and one has won an award, which one do you think will get the most customers?

Make sure you have some victories to talk to your customers about.

#118 If you are confident enough, let your customers try your product

The 'try before you buy' concept is an oldie but a goldie. Luxury car manufacturers use it to great effect. Borrow a new luxury European sports car for a weekend and see how eager you are to give it back on Monday morning.

This is an excellent sales tool. If your product is good enough to speak for itself, your job as a sales person is to get as many people as possible to try it. There are lots of businesses that can use this method—all you need is the confidence to do it.

I did a lot of marketing for a pizza restaurant many years ago. Their claim was that they made the best pizzas in town so every week we set aside a few hours a day to deliver pizzas to local businesses free of charge. We were welcomed with open arms, as anyone dropping off a free gourmet wood-fire pizza would be. In ten years this pizza shop has sold over 300,000 pizzas in a town with a population of just a few thousand people.

I remember walking around the streets of New York City and watching promotional people handing out free samples of shaving cream and toothbrushes. The company's philosophy was that once people tried these products they would keep using them.

I really do recommend this 'put your product where your mouth is' promotion. Selling certainly gets a lot easier when your product is fantastic.

#119 Pick up the cost of the call

Some customers don't care about toll free numbers but I can assure you that many do. More people will ring a toll free number than a long distance number. This is a good enough reason for me to have a toll free number.

While you may not realise it when looking at your monthly phone bill, generally telecommunication is getting cheaper. Pick up the cost of the call and that is one more barrier to buying that you have removed. Often when I recommend this to business owners I see a look of concern on their faces as they imagine their huge phone bills, but a big bill is good because it means people are using the toll free number to buy from you. If no one uses the number there is only a minimal monthly cost.

What is important is to promote the toll free number as a sales hotline or something similar. The most important point I am making with this tip is that getting a toll free number is easy, but it is worthless if nobody knows about it. Remember to put your toll free number on your website, on your brochures, in your advertising and so forth.

#120 Make it really easy for people to pay you

This is a bugbear of mine because I seem to encounter so many businesses that make it really hard to buy from them simply because it is difficult to pay them. If your business doesn't accept pretty much every credit card, you will lose sales every day.

The argument that it is expensive to use cards is old and out of date. Most businesses charge a small percentage to cover the credit card costs and if they don't they are smart enough to absorb the costs to get the sale and to keep the customer happy.

Make sure you have clear signs showing which credit cards you take. On your invoices make this clear and also make sure your bank account details are easy to read and accurate to encourage people to pay you directly.

Long lines at cash registers are crazy. Be innovative—have express lanes, have cash only lanes or anything else that can speed up the process and make it easier for people to pay.

Do whatever you can to make it easy for people to pay you. I like to use one card for all of my business expenses to make it easier for accounting and to collect frequent flyer points. So I avoid businesses that don't take this card. I am sure that I am not the only one in this position.

Talk to your customers. Look for ways to make it easier to accept payments from them or offer flexible payment options of some kind. Most importantly, however, eliminate any obstacles that make it harder for people to buy what you are selling.

#121 Register a clever domain name

Registering descriptive domain names like www.buymorecheese.com or www.aproductthatcanchangeyourlife.com can help to get your website noticed. They are often fun, they make sense and they are generally easy to remember. I think we will see a lot more businesses registering these types of names in the near future so my advice is to spend some time brainstorming the perfect motivating domain name for your products or services.

A key to making this work is to make it really easy to read and remember, like a normal sentence or phrase with .com at the end.

Sounds quirky? It is, but driving sales often needs a little quirk. Go crazy!

20 BONUS TIPS TO HELP YOU SELL MORE OF ANYTHING

Action plan — What can I do right now to become the very best sales person that I can be?

'Only those who have learned the power of sincere and selfless contribution will ever experience life's deepest joy; true fulfilment.'
Anthony Robbins

Where to from here?

Well by now you will have a head full of new ideas (and a few old ones that you might simply have forgotten about) ready to put to use. Keep this book handy, use it often, refer to it if you hit a dry patch and keep developing your skills as an extraordinary sales person.

I welcome any feedback, stories or successes that you might want to pass on. Simply visit my website and drop me an email—www.andrewgriffiths.com.au.

In the meantime, I wish you a truly spectacular amount of success as a sales professional.

Recommended reading

Books

Beckwith, H. *Selling the Invisible*, Warner Business Books, New York, 1997.

Carnegie, D. *How to Win Friends and Influence People*, Harper Collins, New York, 1936.

Connor, T. *91 Mistakes Smart Salespeople Make*, Sourcebooks, Chicago, 2006.

Gitomer, J. *Jeffrey Gitomer's Sales Bible*, HarperCollins, New York, 2008.

Godin, S. *Purple Cow*, Penguin Books, New York, 2003.

Gschwandtner, G. *201 Super Sales Tips*, McGraw Hill, New York, 2006.

Hopkins, T. *How to Master the Art of Selling*, Tom Hopkins International, Scottsdale, 1982.

Pease, A. *Body Language*, Sheldon Press, Sydney, 1997.

Schiffman, S. *The 25 Sales Habits of Highly Successful Sales People*, Adams Media Corporation, Avon MA, 1994.

—— *101 Successful Sales Strategies*, Adams Media Corporation, Avon MA, 2005.

Ziegler, Z. *Selling 101*, Thomas Nelson Inc., Nashville, 2003.

RECOMMENDED READING

Websites

New sales-orientated websites are coming online all the time. I suggest spending time to regularly research online to find resources that you may find useful. The following sites provide good online sales support and advice:

www.business.com
www.entrepreneur.com
www.flyingsolo.com.au
www.marketingprofs.com
www.mysellingskills.com
www.andrewgriffithsblog.com

About the author

Andrew Griffiths is a serial entrepreneur with a passion for helping people achieve their business dreams and goals. He is an internationally renowned business author, dynamic keynote presenter and specialist consultant. But it wasn't always that way.

As an orphan growing up in Western Australia, Andrew survived neglect, abuse and tragedy. In spite of this childhood filled with so many negatives, he grew into a man described as contagiously positive, funny and endlessly enthusiastic. Andrew has taken what life has thrown at him and grown from it rather than letting it overwhelm him.

The one consistent component of Andrew's life has been his dedication to the world of entrepreneurialism. He started his first business at the age of seven when he sold newspapers in the red-light district of Perth. Since then he has gone on to sell encyclopaedias door-to-door, travelled the world as an international sales manager for a large Japanese shipping company, worked in the Great Sandy Desert for a gold exploration company, been a publisher, had his own scuba school and retail shop, and worked as a commercial diver throughout Australia and Papua New Guinea, to mention just a few of his business experiences.

Andrew has founded and run two boutique marketing and corporate communications firms in Australia. Both have

ABOUT THE AUTHOR

developed extensive client networks and his experiences in these firms have been major catalysts in the writing of these books.

Inspired by his desire to see others reach their full potential, Andrew has written eight hugely successful books, with many more on the way. His *101 Ways* business building series offers small business owners practical, smart and realistic advice. The series is now sold in over forty-five countries around the world, in places as diverse as Estonia, Nigeria, China and Iceland.

Known for his ability to entertain, to inspire and to energise, Andrew has become a highly sought-after keynote speaker. His clients are a who's who of the corporate world and he has sold tens of thousands of books to companies using them as either motivational tools for staff or corporate gifts for clients.

Andrew promotes and advocates four key principles in all of the work he does. These are:

The ME myth This is a concept based on the belief that when you stop focusing inwards and start focusing outwards every aspect of your life will improve dramatically.

Inspired communication We live in a world where communication is becoming less personal, more urgent and yet harder to notice. Inspired communication highlights the need for honest interaction and shows how to break down barriers to let any individual or organisation communicate powerfully in the modern world.

The need for the extraordinary Andrew promotes the concept of *extraordinary* being the minimum standard for any business that truly desires exceptional success on every level.

The power of fun Following a trip to India where Andrew witnessed the famous laughing clubs in the streets of Mumbai, it became clear to him that fun is without doubt one of the most powerful tools that any of us can use to have the life we truly want.

Andrew brings each of these ideas to life in his books, in his presentations and in his consulting work. For more information about Andrew Griffiths please visit:

www.andrewgriffiths.com.au
www.andrewgriffithsblog.com
www.bulletproofmybusiness.com
www.thememyth.com

THE *101 WAYS* SERIES

101 WAYS TO MARKET YOUR BUSINESS

Stand out from the crowd.

Here are 101 practical marketing suggestions to help you achieve dramatic improvements in your business without investing a lot of time and money.

Simple, affordable and quick, these innovative tips are easy to implement and will bring you fast results. Choose and apply at least one new idea each week or use this book as a source of inspiration for new ways to market your services, your products and your business itself.

With tips that take just a few moments to read, *101 Ways to Market Your Business* will help you find new customers, increase the loyalty of the customers you already have, create great promotional material and make your business stand out from the crowd.

INCLUDES 20 BONUS SUGGESTIONS TO HELP YOU ATTRACT NEW CUSTOMERS AND KEEP YOUR EXISTING ONES

ISBN 978 1 74175 005 8

THE *101 WAYS* SERIES

101 WAYS TO ADVERTISE YOUR BUSINESS

Read this before you spend another cent on advertising.

Here are 101 proven tips to increase the effectiveness of your advertising. Use these tips to understand what makes one ad work while another fails and you will save a small fortune in wasted advertising.

With tips that take just a few moments to read, *101 Ways to Advertise Your Business* offers step-by-step advice on how to make an advertisement, how to buy advertising space and how to ensure that your advertisement is working to its full potential. Follow the tips and your business will soon be reaping the benefits.

INCLUDES A SPECIAL BONUS SECTION CONTAINING HUNDREDS OF THE BEST ADVERTISING WORDS AND PHRASES

ISBN 978 1 74175 007 2

THE *101 WAYS* SERIES

101 WAYS TO REALLY SATISFY YOUR CUSTOMERS

Simple ways to keep your customers coming back.

Here are 101 practical tips for delivering service that exceeds your customers' expectations and keeps them coming back. In a world where consumers are far more informed, discerning and demanding than ever before, customer service is one of the main areas where a business can outshine its competitors.

Use these simple tips to improve your customer service and you will be well on the way to success and profitability. With tips that take just a few moments to read, *101 Ways to Really Satisfy Your Customers* teaches you to identify what customers expect, and details simple suggestions that will enable your business to exceed these expectations and reap the rewards.

INCLUDES 20 BONUS TIPS THAT WILL REALLY IMPRESS YOUR CUSTOMERS

ISBN 978 1 74175 008 9

THE *101 WAYS* SERIES

101 WAYS TO BOOST YOUR BUSINESS

Energise your business today!

Here are 101 powerful tips to kick-start your business and unlock some of the potential that may be struggling to break through.

With tips that take just a few moments to read, *101 Ways to Boost Your Business* shows you how to make your business better and ultimately more profitable. These no-nonsense tips can be actioned immediately, so you will see results quickly.

These tips cover a host of everyday business issues, and are equally applicable to all industries in each and every corner of the world. They will save you thousands of dollars.

INCLUDES 20 BONUS TIPS THAT WILL RECHARGE YOUR BUSINESS

ISBN 978 1 74175 006 5

THE *101 WAYS* SERIES

101 WAYS TO HAVE A BUSINESS AND A LIFE

Put the passion back into your business and your life.

Is your business all-consuming? Are you tired of feeling overwhelmed every day? Would you like to take control of your life again?

If, like most business owners, you are struggling to balance your business and your life, don't worry! *101 Ways to Have a Business and a Life* provides simple, practical ideas that will help you to identify the reasons behind this lack of balance and what to do about it. Andrew Griffiths has consulted thousands of business owners around the world and compiled their experiences and coping mechanisms into one easy reference book. All of the tips can be implemented quickly and at little or no cost. You can be the boss of your business and your life.

INCLUDES 20 BONUS SUGGESTIONS TO ENSURE THAT YOU'RE THE ONE CALLING THE SHOTS IN YOUR BUSINESS WORLD

ISBN 978 1 74114 787 2

THE *101 WAYS* SERIES

101 WAYS TO BUILD A SUCCESSFUL NETWORK MARKETING BUSINESS

The concept of network marketing is sound: build relationships with like-minded people and sell quality products and services within this network. Some people make amazingly high incomes from their network marketing businesses, but others fall by the wayside. Why do some fail while many prosper?

101 Ways to Build a Successful Network Marketing Business gives smart, practical tips on how to succeed at network marketing. It explains simple and commonsense ways to treat any network marketing business like a mainstream business. By taking away the mystery, it shows you how to turn every venture into a success.

ISBN 978 1 74114 959 3

THE *101 WAYS* SERIES

101 SECRETS TO BUILDING A WINNING BUSINESS

Why do some businesses struggle or even go under, while others go from strength to strength? Generally it has nothing to do with what you're selling, it's all about how you run your business.

Regardless of the industry you're in or the size of your business, *101 Secrets to Building a Winning Business* is packed with practical tips designed to give you the competitive edge.

Renowned small business expert Andrew Griffiths suggests a range of actions that will turn your bright idea into a winning and money-making business. His suggestions are easy to implement, fast, proven and—most importantly—they will not break the bank.

Try out a handful of Andrew's recommendations and you will be on the way to building the business of your dreams.

ISBN 978 1 74175 567 1